For A Great Future: 60 Ready-to-use Assemblies for 21st Century Schools

For A Great Future

60 Ready-to-use Assemblies for 21st Century Schools

Priya Sarin

MEGAGEM

Published by MergageM Sapience
www.megagem.org
gem@megagem.org

ISBN-13: 978-8190889452
ISBN-10: 8190889451

Price: US$ 18.90

Manufactured in the United States of America

Dedicated to those teachers who step up
and become part of the solution

Preface

I was a privileged child. During my formative years I enjoyed a healthy dose of moral values at home and at school. I had the fortune of studying in a values-driven school where school assemblies were invariably a mini class of value education. Unfortunately, many children are not so blessed. Their families and schools want them to excel academically, not holistically. Today, schools are busy in the academic rat race and parents are happy if their children score well in exams. Perhaps they lack time or motivation to impart ethical and moral values. While this series is a humble attempt to overcome the time constraint part of the problem, the motivation part has to come from the school leaders to create a holistic balance between schooling and education.

The academic world is passing through exciting times. The emergence of knowledge economy has ushered in great opportunities. But rapidly changing times also present many challenges. Some of these are serious enough to shake the foundations of our education system if we continue to ignore the crying symptoms. Children's growing indifference towards moral and social values is a serious issue. Most of us believe that ethics are equally, if not more, important than academic knowledge.

One of the fundamental objectives of education is to help children build a strong character and develop a balanced personality. But then, fostering the desirable ethical code has become a secondary issue in our present education system. Education is supposed to instill moral and cultural values. But it appears that education is leading to cultural confusions and a confusing culture. Prospicient people shudder to think what is in store for our future generations if the decline in moral values continues.

Study after study is pointing to a continual decline in moral values.

But sadly the emphasis of education is increasingly shifting from the ethics based nurturing to the curriculum-centric teaching. The competitive dimensions are taking centre stage in our education system, which churns out a few winners at the expense of majority. While teaching and nurturing are interrelated and intertwined, they are not the same. Their elements as well as objectives are different. So, it is important to differentiate between teaching and nurturing. And both should get their due place. But of late, teaching is getting more and more importance at the expense of nurturing.

Most of us appreciate that the process of education should not be limited to imparting knowledge and developing skills; it should also aim at evolving the individual as a complete person, who can think rationally and behave responsibly. And it is not important what is poured into the pupil, but what is planted that really matters in the ultimate analysis.

This series intends to help teachers to take advantage of school assemblies to creatively engage students in matters important to the future of humanity. This book contains thirty modules, each containing one storytelling session and one give-and-take session. I have given special attention to enhance the psychological impact of the material, many times even at the expense of syntax. The mandate I have followed is to keep it interesting and absorbing so that children can subconsciously internalize the desired values. But sometimes, in the debate of making the material interesting or important to the cause, my primary objective compelled me to focus on the importance aspect.

On a personal note, I express my grateful gratitude to my teachers, friends and family members for inspiring me with their moral support. I hope teachers will find this book useful and oblige me with their valuable suggestions to further improve the book.

May God be with you in your endeavor to light up the lives of tomorrow's citizens.

Priya Sarin
feedback@foragreatfuture.com

Contents

Index of Key and Supplementary Values

Value	Value Links as	
	Key Values (Module #)	Supplementary Values (Module #)
Abstinence	8, 14	22
Appreciating Fantasy vs. Reality	18	
Appreciating the Family Love	2, 19, 20	27
Avoiding Drugs	22, 27	
Avoiding Plagiarism		6
Balance	11	16, 28, 30
Caring	16	20, 26
Caring for Elders	4	
Common Cause		13
Compassion	1, 20	2
Concern for Others		21
Cooperation		16, 23, 25
Courtesy		1
Democratic Decision Making	28	
Dignity of the Individual		25
Discipline	29	

| Value | Value Links as | |
	Key Values (Module #)	Supplementary Values (Module #)
Duty		4, 8
Empathy		1, 2
Equality	25	21
Faithfulness		14
Forgiveness		14
Forward Looking	3	8, 13
Friendship	9, 23, 26	10, 24
Giving		20
Good Manners		24
Gratitude	4	5, 26
Healthy Eating	7	11
Healthy Living	11, 12	7
Helpfulness	26	29
Honesty	22	21
Humanism		5, 21, 25
Humility	3, 10, 24	
Imagination		28
Initiative		15, 16
Integrity	6, 21, 23	3
Justice		23
Kindness		21
Kindness to Animals		6, 7, 22

Value	Value Links as	
	Key Values (Module #)	Supplementary Values (Module #)
Knowing Oneself	10	
Managing Peer Pressure	15, 17, 19	12, 24, 27
Modesty		10
Obedience		18, 27
Peace		2
Perseverance	8, 14	28
Positive Thinking	7	
Presence of Mind		1
Proper Utilization of Time	30	
Quest for Knowledge	6, 8, 28	
Reasonableness		18
Regularity		30
Respect for Others		25
Respect for Parents	27	
Respect for the Environment	13	9, 23
Responsibility to Family	16, 29	
Responsibility to Friends	9	
Responsibility to Parents	5	
Responsibility to Self	12, 15, 29	3, 16
Reverence for Old Age		4
Self-esteem	19	11
Self-motivation		19

Value	Value Links as	
	Key Values (Module #)	Supplementary Values (Module #)
Self-discipline	30	8, 9
Self-reliance	16	14, 15, 29
Self-restraint		17, 18, 24
Sense of Good and Bad	2	
Sense of Right and Wrong	15, 17, 18	3, 12, 19
Sharing		20, 23
Simple Living	24	11, 13, 17
Social Responsibility	1, 13, 21	
Team Spirit		9, 28
Tolerance	25	5
Truthfulness		6
Unconditional Love	5	29
Willpower		7, 8
Wisdom		10

Index of Life Skills

Life Skill	Module #
Balance	5, 20
Career Planning	15
Caring	21
Common Sense	10, 17
Cooperation	13
Courage	1, 14
Creative Thinking	8, 28
Decision Making	3, 15
Devotion	8, 14
Discipline	16, 17, 27
Fairness	25
Flexibility	4, 5, 27
Forward Looking	11, 14
Friendship	12, 25
General Knowledge	13, 24
Giving	21
Good Habits	5, 7, 26, 27
Good Manners	9, 11, 12, 25
Hard Work	6, 8, 23

Life Skill	Module #
Healthy Body Image	11
Helpfulness	2
Independence	19
Initiative	1, 2, 8, 28
Integrity	22, 23
Organizing	20, 29, 30
Perseverance	23
Planning and Organizing	16
Planning for the Future	3, 13
Problem Solving	28
Quest for Knowledge	10
Respect for Elders	4
Self-awareness	3, 12, 22
Self-control	7, 9, 20, 24, 27
Self-discipline	18, 19
Self-help	6, 29, 30
Sharing	13, 21
Team Work	9
Thinking Skills	7
Thriftiness	24
Time Management	16, 26, 29, 30
Tolerance	4
Willpower	18, 19, 24
Writing Skills	6

The Art of Storytelling

God has given some special abilities to humans. Storytelling is one of them. The practice of sharing ideas, knowledge and wisdom through stories is a time-honored tradition in every culture. In fact, storytelling is as old as speech itself. It is not only the oldest form of education, but also an effective medium to open the minds of listeners, especially children.

The art of storytelling continues to flourish as we tell stories to children to entertain them, engage them, and pass on knowledge and values to them. Anyone can read a story but, when a story is effectively told, children are more likely to retain it because it goes straight to the heart. Good stories stick with children. Storytelling is a good tool to leverage the teaching-learning process because students enjoy storytelling and often become emotionally involved in the process. Neil Gaiman beautifully describes the importance of stories by saying, "Tales and dreams are the shadow-truths that will endure when mere facts are dust and ashes, and forgotten."

What differentiates humans from other creatures is the fact that we can listen to other people's stories and tell them our stories. In fact, we all live to tell stories. It's our natural way to share information. But what does it take to tell a story that entertains children and appeals to their moral sense. Effective storytelling is much more than simply communicating a story in an entertaining way. It's an opportunity to bring children into the narrative so that they can relate with the story and its characters. It's an opportunity to engage children with the underlying message. It's an effective way to instill moral values in children.

We all tell stories, but some are better at it than others. Everyone has a story to tell, but not everyone has the confidence to tell stories to a large group of listeners or to the school in assembly. Initially, it may seem a bit daunting to people unfamiliar with the art of storytelling. While mastering the art of storytelling is not an easy task, but it is not that difficult as well. Once you learn the tricks and practice this art, you'd be amazed at how easy it is to tell a story effectively, and how eager children are to hear what you have to say. There are some simple storytelling techniques which can enhance the impact of a story. When you use good storytelling techniques, you can turn an ordinary story into an extraordinary experience.

Good storytellers have a magical ability to mesmerize listeners. Good storytellers can spark, stir, or create an emotional connection between their listeners and the characters of their stories. They can do this because humans have a natural tendency to relate with others. A good story and a good storyteller can prove that 'one plus one equals eleven'. They are more than simply the sum of their parts.

We all know how to tell a story. And we all know how to walk. Yet almost all aspiring models take lessons to learn how to walk on the ramp. Likewise, it is important for a storyteller to relearn and practice the art of storytelling. Anyone can improve the storytelling skill by watching experienced storytellers and taking to heart some basic tips and techniques. And practice is also very important; it makes you better. Here are some simple tips and hints to potentiate your storytelling potential.

Most teachers are familiar with the art of storytelling techniques, and they appreciate their importance. They also know how these techniques can make the storytelling session a memorable experience when they are balanced, harmonized and enlivened by each other. Even the following factors are not new to them; it is just that they tend to overlook them in their daily drudgery. So here, we take up some deceptively ordinary yet definitely important tips to improve the art of storytelling.

Own the story: Good storytelling demands preparation. You should read the story several times and live with it until the characters and settings become familiar. After wisely evaluating the story and acquainting yourself with the narrative, you should decide to use the story as it is or make some subtle changes, minor alterations, or major changes in line with your objective. While minor changes are desirable, it is not recommended to alter the shape or structure of the tale. But you must make the story yours in whatever way suits you best. Here are some ideas to learn your story by heart.

- use story skeletons to help you remember the plot
- recount yourself the story in your own words to appreciate the shape of the tale
- try to view the story as a movie to own the narrative
- adapt and improvise the narrative to retell it creatively
- repeat it until you are happy about it

Know your voice: Your greatest tool as a storyteller is your voice. So, it is imperative to first know what kind of voice you have. Do you whisper or boom? Do you trudge like a turtle or race like a rabbit? Do you agitate or orchestrate?

Your voice is the main tool that you rely upon in storytelling. If your voice is not in optimum condition, then your storytelling performance may suffer. While it is important to maintain the natural quality of your voice, it is also important to put emotion into the sound, as this will add emotional color to your story. The way you modulate your voice, stress words and phrases, and pause for effect depicts your emotions and induces a reactive emotion in your audience. This reactive emotion is what draws children into the story. They live through the story and remain absorbed in it, away from the real world, fascinated and enthralled by your voice. Here are some tips for making the most of this key element.

Regulate the volume: Consciously adjust your volume suitably to stir listeners' interest and to prevent your voice from slipping into monotony. While it is important to regulate the volume, you should always speak loud enough to be clearly heard.

Refine the pitch: Pitch is the frequency of the sound waves we produce. Although sound waves travel through air at a fairly constant speed, the frequency with which they are released makes the sound higher or lower. A consistent pitch leads to monotony. We tend to pay no heed to sounds with no variation. Using low and high pitch alternately will keep your audience's attention. Varying your pitch intelligently gives your story energy and momentum.

Change the rhythm and pace: Rhythm is the order and arrangement of sounds and silence over a period of time. It is simply the pattern of the sounds you produce. Use it effectively to convey the message. Change the pace to slow to emphasize certain ideas and intensify it to show excitement or humor. Slow the pace or use a brief silence to give audience the time to absorb a tricky point or when you move to another idea. It will allow your listeners to digest your message.

Control the timbre: It is the color and emotional quality of your voice. Timber is the attitude behind your narrative. Listeners perceive a storyteller's attitude, and use their perception to understand the narrative. To add meaning to the story and connect with the listeners, use it optimally to express the emotions and feelings.

Use the pause: One of the easiest ways to experiment with voice variety is to use a very brief break. A pause before or after a key point indicates the importance of the point in an effective manner. It also gets the audience's attention as they can use this break to process what you have just said.

Most storytellers underestimate how their voice can enhance the impact of their story. Using vocal variety keeps children engaged and spices up your narrative. A monotone delivery will fail to connect with children. So, avoid a flat or monotone delivery at all costs. Try to keep your delivery somewhat deliberate. An expressive voice that explores its range, rhythm, pace and volume will quickly bring a story to life. Remember, if your voice comes across as ordinary, the audience will perceive your story and message as being ordinary as well.

Performance skills: Storytelling means relating a tale to listeners through voice and expressions. While voice is crucial, all your non-verbal expressions and gestures are equally important to improve your performance. Good storytellers know how to selectively use the following traits to emotionally engage children.

- Use their face, body and gestures
- Maintain eye contact with the listeners
- Adjust their attitude and enthusiasm to fit the story and message
- Make their actions respond to the tale
- Have a clear focus and maintain concentration
- Make the audience believe in them
- Use their space to create a charismatic presence
- Expressively use non-verbal communication to clarify the meaning of the text

It is better to stand while you are telling a tale. If you stand during your storytelling session, your voice may sound broader and more confident. When you sit, your voice may not project as well and you may have a tendency to sound too relaxed. While it's not always true and every individual is different, generally storytellers find that standing helps them convey their story in a more compelling way.

Great storytellers know how to engage their listeners. They know how to stimulate all five senses and create memorable moments for their audience. Great storytellers know what they want to say; they think what they mean; they express what they feel; they always remember to regain their natural style as a narrator.

Storytelling is one of the most important tools for teaching moral values. However, good teachers are not necessarily good storytellers, but they do share certain traits. Both are self-aware, and both are intellectuals who realize that teaching or preaching is not about what you say; it's about what listeners remember.

Storytelling is a skill. People are not born with this skill. They develop it gradually. When they refine their verbal and non-verbal skills through reflection and practice, their stories strike a chord with the audience. They become adept at taking audience from nowhere to somewhere in an exhilarating journey through an enticing mix of entertainment and wisdom. Nancy Mellon, founder of the school of therapeutic storytelling says, "Because there is a natural storytelling urge and ability in all human beings, even just a little nurturing of this impulse can bring about astonishing and delightful results." In fact, learning to tell stories in the assembly or classroom is a very worthwhile and satisfying experience for teachers.

At the end of the day, storytelling is just a good communication at work. What's different about it is that there are some techniques to make your story effective, memorable and enjoyable. These techniques help you practice the process so that you can incorporate it seamlessly into your own, natural style.

Effective Give-and-Take Sessions

In today's world, value crisis is not an exception. It is casting its evil shadow in all walks of our life. The continuous decline in moral and ethical values of our society is baffling the minds of all. We all wonder why so many young people resort to unethical means and immoral ways to get what they want. In view of the continuous decline in the moral quotient of children, it would not be wrong to assume that the archaic and regimented way of teaching has somewhat failed to achieve the objectives of holistic education.

Children are like wet clay, whoever touches them, makes an impression. They can be molded in any way. What's more, children are quick learners and naturally absorb the world around them. They intuitively imbibe values from their parents, teachers and friends. That's why they say that values are more 'caught' than 'taught'.

If you have seen cartoons, you may recall a tiny red devil who sat on the shoulder of many characters. This little devil whispered bad advice and nasty ideas into the character's ear – prodding him to do the wrong thing. Believe it or not, we all have a devil sitting on our shoulders. And he can really mess up our thinking if the white angel sitting on our other shoulder doesn't control the devil.

We all have two sides, good and bad. And what we choose to follow defines who we really are. God does not have much influence on whether good or bad things happen to us. God gave us free will, and we are creators of our own destiny.

One of the key objectives of give-and-take sessions is to strengthen the good side and encourage a healthy debate between the good and the bad side whenever impressionable minds are tempted by the bad side. And it is important since the bad side is gaining strength from the onslaught of screen culture in the lives of children.

A young mind is highly sensitive and susceptible to negative influences assailing it from outside. Now-a-days the role and scope of these negative influences is assuming alarming proportions owing to ever-increasing penetration of the newer synthetic mediums in the lives of children. The evolution of screen culture and the decline in moral values may not be a mere coincidence. The earlier laidback approach may have worked in relatively static and less complex times, but it could prove quite damaging in these rapidly changing environments where newer technologies are penetrating the protective walls of homes and schools.

Therefore, teachers' role in shaping the society needs to be expanded to deal with the rapidly changing landscape of various types of temptations. To counteract the impact of modern negative influences on children, education should be a tool not just for employment but also for empowerment. And teachers need to take responsibility for students' empowerment in the true sense in addition to their learning and employment. Now, it is more than ever imperative for teachers and parents to mold children so that they grow up to become good human beings.

So then, how do we instill values and develop character in schoolchildren? We have tried to integrate values into curriculum, but still do not know how to make that work. Here the effort to reward ratio is nowhere near reasonable, particularly considering the fact that teachers usually feel pressed to make every minute count. Once I told some school students that eighty percent of the students seem uninterested in the value education class. They replied that I had underestimated the percentage. Educators and experts agree that it is easy to agree about the importance of teaching values, but finding a practical, result-oriented model to truly provide a holistic education is the real challenge.

In view of this, a time-efficient and effective way of imparting values to tomorrow's citizens was envisaged to supplement the ongoing efforts. Accordingly, the give-and-take sessions are designed to intrigue the minds of children as well as touch their hearts. While it is a challenge to effectively conduct the give-and-take sessions in school assemblies due to time constraints, it offers a golden opportunity to promote values and positive attitudes in an effective and efficient manner.

A give-and-take session is meant to be a powerful collection of words of wisdom that inspire, educate, enlighten and motivate a child to take action. For our purpose, a give-and-take session may be defined as the continuous deliberation of something, or about something for some time. It is a dialogue with self and others, a sharing of ideas and information, and mutual questioning. It is a process which we undertake to internalize good behaviors. While it is not a one-sided initiative, it may appear so in the school assemblies where often students are expected to deliberate silently due to time constraints.

Children need to be reminded of the values again and again so as to make these their second nature. But how to make the process really effective? When we remind them 'honesty is the best policy', they listen it, but their brain does not process it. So, repeating it doesn't serve the intended purpose. Perhaps we are wasting their time. Trust me, they really think so. But then, how we could ingrain the fear of insects in the young minds with 90% success rate whereas in the case of scruples, we are seriously lacking behind. And we should earnestly think about why statements like 'Honesty is not always the best policy' or 'When helping the wounded, honesty is secondary to healing' strike a chord with today's children and stand a better chance in the game of nurturing them.

A teacher's typical mindset is proprietary mindset whereas the present times require collaborative mindset. When it comes to value education, a collaborative mindset is imperative to encourage and enable children to construct moral values for themselves. This approach invariably promises better outcomes.

While the modules presented in the book are ready to use in class or school assemblies, it is always better to suitably modify them according to the students' needs. It is not difficult. Teachers just need to spend some time to assess the needs of the students and try to add/delete/modify the content according to time availability so as to make it more interesting and enlightening. Here are some helpful hints to make a give-and-take session more effective.

✓ Subtle approach: In view of the fact that values are more 'caught' than 'taught', it is always better to adopt a subtle approach. While it may be a bit difficult to comprehend or integrate it in your plan, it is the most effective and result-oriented way to impart value education. So, try to maintain an optimum balance between direct and subtle approach.

✓ Points to ponder: It is not necessary for students to answer the questions or participate in the discussion. They are just required to ponder over them. Sometimes, you may encourage them to imagine a white angel and a red devil sitting on their shoulders and debating between themselves. And remind them that the devil represents temptation and the angel represents conscience. So, after every question or statement, a brief pause is suggested so as to allow their subconscious mind to absorb the desired values. This is recommended only for school assemblies where time for the give-and-take session is limited. This pointer is reminded in every fifth module.

✓ Involve them: If practical, encourage students and colleagues in the storytelling session to suggest a similar story, preferably a local story or real life example. The teacher-coordinator should guide and give the time or words limit. Before using it in the give-and-take session, the coordinator should review it in the light of key values. Also points to ponder should be re-examined and suitably modified.

✓ Engage them: Teachers should encourage students to discuss the issues with their friends, teachers and family members as well as with themselves. Encourage tech-obsessed children to use social networks to engage others in the exchange of ideas. This can be a great way to positively engage students as well as ensure that they retain what they have learned. I have intentionally left some open-ended debates to offer intellectual fodder to the intelligent students so as to creatively engage them. Moreover, teachers should sportingly take students' comments or criticism.

✓ Follow 'Learn-it-all' approach: A sense of curiosity is nature's original school of education. So wherever possible, some time should be given for silent contemplation to the students. A give-and-take session should be less of a preaching and more of an engaging, fun interaction. Emphasis should be more on 'learn-it-all' approach in preference to 'teach it all' approach.

✓ Make it more relevant: To enhance the impact quotient and relevancy of the material, teachers may change words, language, etc. according to the students' and regional needs.

✓ Variety: Teachers can incorporate a variety of things to keep students entertained and involved. For example, share a personal experience, relate the topic to previously covered content, use an interesting quotation, relate the theme to future life experiences, and the like. At the end of each session, teachers may leave behind a pinch of suspense to make the students curious, which will motivate them to explore more.

✓ Be a facilitator: Teachers should not consider a give-and-take session on value education as another subject to be taught to students, but rather as an opportunity for healthy, vibrant recreation while offering experiential, empowering and contextually relevant content. Your role should be less of a teacher and more of a facilitator, initiator and coordinator. Your session will be more productive if you conduct it with a positive mindset of a learner, in preference to a teacher's mindset.

✓ Get ready: Here are some other basic points to remember in preparing and presenting a give-and-take session.
  ➢ Make sure to be well-prepared before presenting the session
  ➢ Avoid eating a big meal before your session
  ➢ Keep in mind that you have to attract others' attention
  ➢ Make sure that your speed is proper when you talk to people, not too fast or slow
  ➢ Talk friendly and politely. Smile often and enjoy

While the learned readers know the above-mentioned points and much more to make the give-and-take sessions really effective, it is just that they tend to take them lightly as there is no reliable yardstick to measure their impact. Moreover, the tips discussed above do not make an exhaustive list. They are selected on the strength of their potential to enhance the psychological impact of the give-and-take sessions. Besides, they may be deficient in scope as the inputs are limited to my experience, which is insignificant considering the enormity of the challenge.

The objective of education is not to merely load the minds of students with facts; it is to teach them to think rationally. The curriculum is important, but thinking and real life skills are equally important. The renowned educational researcher and teacher educator John Goodlad of the University of Washington says that we spend less than one percent of teaching time asking students to reason and think. We expect them to just regurgitate rather than reason and think. The give-and-take sessions are designed to encourage students to reason and think so as to maximize the psychological impact of the exercise. The objective is to prompt them to establish an emotional connect with the moral themes. It is a simple but an endearing and enduring approach since the themes are carefully selected to encourage children to reflect and arrive at their own conclusions. I hope this deceptively ordinary approach, where you facilitate children to think about moral values and guide them to develop their own beliefs, will help you to achieve extraordinary success in the domain of value education.

As guardian of the future of humanity, remember Proverbs 22:6 says that teaching a child something over and over is the best way to ensure that it sticks with him as an adult.

To check story/module wise pointers on the give-and-take sessions, please refer www.foragreatfuture.com

1. The Crying Girl

Purpose of the module: It aims to encourage children to develop a sense of compassion and the ability to empathize. The goal is to make the students aware of their responsibility to the society and encourage them to look beyond the obvious.

Key Values: Compassion, Sense of Social Responsibility.
Supplementary Values: Empathy, Presence of Mind, Courtesy.
Life Skills: Courage, Initiative.
Estimated Storytelling Time: 6 to 8 Minutes
Give-and-Take Session: 5 to 9 Minutes

Ron and his friends were watching a movie. Suddenly Ron got a call. He thought that his mother was calling him for something important. He went out to take the call. On the other end, there was a baby crying and saying, "Daddy, momma is not waking."

He realized that the baby was trying to call her father but by mistake called him. He asked her who she was. She said, "Ginny. Momma not waking up."

He sweetly asked her where her mother was.

She stammered, "Momma sleeping on the bathroom floor."

Ron panicked and asked her what was wrong. When he got no reply, he again asked her where she lived.

She blurted, "Home."

Controlling his anxiety, Ron again gently asked her, "I mean where is your home located?"

She was crying a lot. In between her cries, she uttered, "Don't know."

Ron replied, "Don't worry baby. I am coming."

He went back to his friends and told them everything. They laughed at his panicky look and said, "Come on Ron, you know it was just a prank call. Someone from our school must have got his younger sister to call and tell you that."

Ron persisted, "But even if there's just a one per cent chance, I would like to take it."

He immediately went out and dialed the telecom operator's number. After waiting for 5 minutes and wasting another 3 minutes on the automated voice response system, he could finally talk to someone on the line. He requested her to give him the address of that phone number. Operator told him that it was against their company's policy to disclose address to anyone. He explained to her the situation, but she was firm. Like his friends, she also told him that it was just a prank call. When he argued what if it was a real emergency, she told him that the neighbors would take care of it and he should not worry unnecessarily. He realized that she was an Asian replying from a call centre in India. Perhaps, she would not understand the value of life.

Ron got into his car and went to the phone company's nearest office. There he demanded to meet the manager. The manager was busy and his secretary came to meet him. Ron thought that talking to the secretary would only waste time, so he insisted on meeting the manager urgently. The manager was in a meeting. Ron stormed into their room. He told the manager that he must give him the address of that number. The manager got irritated and said, "I can't give you the address. We have a privacy policy."

Hoping that better sense would prevail on the manager, Ron again narrated the story briefly and urged, "Just call on this number once and you will realize what I am saying is true."

The manager who wanted to get rid of Ron as soon as possible dialed the number. No one picked it. He said, "Satisfied now? They are not even picking the phone. They must have gone out or something. Everyone has busy lives young man. Now please excuse me."

Ron requested him to call again as it could be a matter of life or death for someone. The manager realized that Ron was stubborn. He redialed the number just to get rid of him quickly. This time someone picked up. The manager became concerned and tried talking to the child, but could not get any further information as the child was just sobbing. He immediately called his secretary and told him to give the address of this number urgently.

As the secretary went to retrieve the address from the computer, the manager turned to Ron and said, "This number series belongs to New York City. Let's move. My secretary will tell us the exact location on the way."

They went on the manager's bike as time was of essence. In five minutes, the secretary called and told them the exact address. They went to Ginny's home and started knocking. As Ginny was not able to open the door, they had to break it. When they got inside, they went to the bathroom and saw that Ginny was crying and trying to wake up her mother. Her mother was lying on the floor unconscious. They rushed her to a nearby hospital where the doctors performed a by-pass surgery on her. She had suffered a massive heart attack.

When Ginny's father came, he profusely thanked both of them for their efforts. Ron was really happy that his presence of mind could save a life. Next day, the story and Ron's photo appeared in the newspapers. Ron's parents and teachers were proud of him, and rightfully so.

The governor declared him Hero of the Year for his compassionate act, and the phone company gifted him the latest iPhone7 with free phone service for life.

Ron's father smiled through his tears and proudly remarked, "We have passed the parenting exam with flying colors."

Give-and-Take Session

Compassion is the quality that makes us human. Compassion is not just being emotional and feeling for someone. That's sympathy, not compassion. Compassion requires action, which seeks to change the situation. When a reflex reaction makes us to help an unfamiliar person, with no motivation other than that the person is in need, empathy or compassion is in action.

Even the smallest thing that we do for others can bring about a great change in the world. We may not get to see the change at once, but every good action surely has its reward. So we should always try to behave in such a way that our actions will benefit others. Even a smile is very valuable. And it costs us nothing, but gives a lot. A smile enriches those who receive it without making poorer those who give it.

Mother Teresa was a humanitarian who devoted her life to helping the poor, sick and orphaned. She was an example of 'compassion in action' and someone who took responsibility for her part in the solution.

In 1948, Mother Teresa left her teaching post at a Roman Catholic Girls' School in Kolkata in order to devote her life to working among the poorest of the poor in the slums of Kolkata. Mother Teresa pioneered a new way of looking at the poor, hungry and sick of our world. Her teachings of spreading love throughout the world in order to give the poor the simple dignity of human recognition and love were groundbreaking. She inspired the world with her example of compassion for the poor, and set a standard unequaled in the twentieth century. She was awarded the 1979 Nobel Peace Prize for her humanitarian work.

Her teachings were simple, short and sweet. She touched the hearts of people around the world inspiring hope and understanding through her teachings of compassion and love. When Mother Teresa received the Nobel Peace Prize, she was asked, "What can we do to promote world peace?"

She answered "Go home and love your family."

Points to Ponder
(It is not necessary for students to answer the questions or participate in discussion. They are just required to ponder over them. So, after every question or statement, a brief pause is recommended so as to allow their subconscious mind to absorb the desired values.)

- Ginny, a toddler was seeking help for her mother. Was it 'compassion in action'? *pause...* Why?
- Had you been in Ron's place, what would you have done?
- Riding a bike in the city is dangerous. Why the manager went on his bike to Ginny's house?
- Why Ron broke down a stranger's front door?
- Ron's parents said, "We have passed the parenting game with flying colors." What does it mean?
- Teaching is a caring profession, which also requires compassion as a skill. Then why did Mother Teresa leave the teaching job?
- There is no Nobel Prize category for compassion or working for poor. Then why Mother Teresa was given a Nobel award?
- Would you like to become a compassionate person? Why?
- How does one actually become a compassionate person?
- Would you like to become a socially responsible citizen?
- Do you think you have a sense of social responsibility?

Compassion is the tie that binds every human being. So be compassionate when you can, try to understand what people are going through and do your best to be there for them.

Love and compassion are necessities, not luxuries. Without them humanity cannot survive. Humanity depends on love and compassion. Live, love and be happy, and make others so.

2. Brain Is King, Heart Is Queen

Purpose of the module: This story aims to create an appreciation of the nurturing atmosphere of family and make children sensitive to the feelings and needs of others. It is important to make children understand the difference between feeling 'for' others and feeling 'with' others.

Key Values: Sense of Discrimination between Good and Bad, Family Love.
Supplementary Values: Empathy, Compassion, Peace.
Life Skills: Helpfulness, Initiative.
Estimated Storytelling Time: 6 to 8 Minutes
Give-and-Take Session: 5 to 10 Minutes

Lizzie was a student of 11th grade. She had to submit a report on the functioning of the brain. She was reading a big book on the topic. Her kid brother Matt, who was six years old, came and climbed on her bed. In her father's tone, Matt questioned her, "What are you doing? Why you skipped lunch?"

Lizzie sweetly replied, "I am researching about the brain and its functions for my psychology assignment. I must complete it today as I have to present it tomorrow. I feel sleepy after lunch. That's why I skipped lunch."

Matt was a bit confused, wondering how anyone could skip a pizza lunch. Trying to mask his surprise, he countered back, "What exactly you have to write?"

Lizzie said, "I have to write a report on how the brain works. Why do different people think differently?"

Matt assured her, "Don't worry. I will help you. You take some cookies and coke. I will write a good report for you."

Lizzie lovingly smiled and said, "Ok. You also write something and I will include it in my file."

Matt was happy to help and ran to his room. He was busy in his room for two hours. It was a record for super naughty Matt who loved to compete with Dennis the Menace. When he came out at suppertime, he looked very satisfied. He ran to Lizzie and gave her his report. She thanked him and told him she would read it in front of the whole class.

Next day after Lizzie read her report, she requested the teacher, "If you allow, I would also like to read a report that my six-year-old brother has written on this topic to help me."

All students got excited. It's not just that the curious students were welcoming a change from the boring class. They were also eager to see this topic from a six-year-old kid's perspective.

After the teacher's permission, Lizzie read out Matt's report on brain:
1. Our brain is king of all organs. Since it is the king, it stays at the top in our head.
2. Brain is very hard working. It works all the time.
3. My brain is responsible for functioning of all my body parts. While it treats heart as queen, it loves all of them equally. It does not show favoritism.
4. My brain controls my heart in which all my friends and family live. My brain tells me to love them all.
5. When my family or friends need help, my brain helps me in giving them suggestions, and writing reports for Lizzie. My brain likes to do Lizzie's homework, especially when I get her share of pizza.
6. My brain is weird. Whenever someone is hurt or sad, it makes my heart feel the pain. Sometimes, my brain becomes numb during the exam for which I have not prepared.
7. My brain becomes excited whenever something new and interesting happens.

8. God has given everyone in my class the same brain, but only some use it and get good grades. I use it whenever I have time. More girls get good grades than boys. I don't know why God has made girls good at using it.
9. Daddy says, "In every brain there are good thoughts and bad thoughts. To become a champ, you just have to learn to control the bad ones." I don't like people who don't control their bad thoughts. Because of them, we have bad things like violence and terrorism.
10. In every brain, many good things like love and hope live. We should not harm them. The brain gets upset when we do that and makes us cry.

Everyone was shocked and surprised. The teacher with moist eyes started clapping in appreciation of Matt's views on the brain. She then said, "Since the brain and heart are both powerful forces, each one wanting to be the boss over the other, we find it difficult to truly connect them. Children know how to harmonize their brain and heart. Matt's report is a proof of this fact. Our education system gives so much emphasis on educating the brain that the heart is simply overlooked. Children are God's creation. They are born wise. Our education system and upbringing spoil some of them. It is because some parents consider bringing up children a burden, and some teachers consider teaching profession just a way to earn livelihood."

She paused to wipe the tears from her eyes and concluded with the famous words of Emma Goldman: "No one has yet realized the wealth of sympathy, the kindness and generosity hidden in the soul of a child. The effort of every true education should be to unlock that treasure."

The whole class was clapping for little Matt who really understood the brain's primary role in our life.

Give-and-Take Session

Albert Einstein famously said that "Few are those who see with their own eyes and feel with their own hearts."

Considered one of the greatest minds of modern times, Albert Einstein was a scientist who won the Nobel Prize for Physics. Einstein was not just a scientific genius, he was also much more. His curiosity was endless, and he considered imagination his most important scientific tool. Einstein believed in magic. Nature inspired him to research deeply into the mysteries of life. He was a true science hero, not only because of his scientific genius, but also because of his philosophy and compassion for the universe and its creatures.

People tend to think that scientists use more of brain as compared to heart, and artists use more of heart as compared to brain. That's not true. Most wise people make balanced use of heart and head.

Once, Einstein took a decision from his mind ignoring humanitarian aspects, which he regretted later. On the eve of World War II, he feared that Germany might be developing an atomic weapon. Though a peace lover, he urged the then President Franklin Roosevelt to develop an atomic bomb before Hitler did. But when the United States dropped the atomic bombs on the Japanese cities of Hiroshima and Nagasaki, killing more than 115,000 people, he regretted this decision taken from his mind, not his heart. He later called this the biggest mistake of his career.

Points to Ponder

- Empathy means to show that you care and are sensitive to the feelings and the needs of others. Caring people show empathy and selfish people lack empathy. Do you agree?
- Why Matt offered to help Lizzie with her homework? ...*pause*... Was it because of family love or empathy or pizza?
- Why Matt feels the pain of others?
- Matt thinks that God has made girls good at using brain. Do you agree?
- How can we show empathy for others?
- How does the lack of empathy affect us?

- Is the teacher right in saying that kids know how to balance guidance from brain and heart?
- Do children know right from wrong when it comes to junk food or other unhealthy habits?
- Your school makes every effort to give a balanced emphasis on knowledge (brain) and wisdom (heart). How can we further fine-tune this balance?
- Albert Einstein said, "Everything that can be counted does not necessarily count; everything that counts cannot necessarily be counted." What does it mean?

The great physicist Richard Feynman once said that the easiest person to fool is yourself. He further added that one has to be particularly careful to find out not only what is right about one's beliefs and ideas but also what could be wrong with them. If we all followed this in everyday life, we can easily make positive changes in our lives. But we do not. We tend to stick with what we accept as true.

The world's best-known critical thinker, Dr. Michael Shermer says that we just believe things, and then make our world fit our perceptions. He asserts that the human brain is a belief engine, and beliefs come first and explanations for beliefs follow. This somewhat irrational behavior of our brain can be counterproductive to our personal growth, success and happiness. So, it is really important to clearly recognize what is working for you, and to keep doing more of that. It is also important to know what is not working for you, and do your best to get rid of that.

The ability to decide between good and bad or right from wrong is learned. And to make a right decision between good and bad, one needs to use both brain and heart. The most common quality of successful people is that they can strike a balance between brain and heart. They can control their thinking.

When you take complete control over your thinking, you gain control over other aspects of your life. But sometimes our brain says one thing and our heart says another, and we don't know what to do. We may follow one or the other and then regret our decision.

What if we could get a balanced guidance from both brain and heart?

Do you want to find a balance between your heart and your mind? You can, but that requires practice and willpower.

3. The Career Dilemma

Purpose of the module: It aims to make the students aware of responsibility to self and develop their sense of discrimination between right and wrong. It also seeks to underline the importance of humility and forward-looking approach. And encourage students to judiciously think how they can draw on their latent talents in a responsible way.

Key Values: Forward Looking, Humility.
Supplementary Values: Responsibility to Self, Integrity, Sense of Right and Wrong.
Life Skills: Self-awareness, Planning for the Future, Decision Making.
Estimated Storytelling Time: 7 to 9 Minutes
Give-and-Take Session: 5 to 10 Minutes

The 8th grade students were very excited. It was the day of career pop quiz. The quiz was designed to tell them what career would suit them considering their talents and interests. Sarah and her friend Amy were busy guessing what results they would get.

Sarah asked Amy, "What do you think we will get? I want a career with a good paycheck and lots of power."

Amy looked up at her and thoughtfully replied, "That's not right Sarah. You should focus on your talents and abilities. That way success is guaranteed."

Sarah wanted power to boss over everybody else. She casually explained, "With power, I will get the ability to get things done. Whatever I won't be able to do, I will simply delegate."

The bell rang. Both of them hurried to the class. The test was simple. It consisted of questions like your future goals, your hobbies, your preferences and some academic questions to judge student's talents.

The teacher instructed them to answer all the questions honestly. They should not be biased towards a particular career. They should not answer based on what they would like to do. Sarah was biased towards a powerful and money-minting career. She always wanted to become a politician. She tried hard to attempt the quiz in a way that was sure to get her desired result.

When the results were announced, Sarah got financial advisor as the most suitable career option for her. She hated accounts. Although she scored good marks in it, she considered it a boring subject meant for clerks. There was no way that she would like to become a financial advisor.

She decided to talk to the school counselor Mr. Harry. He was a considerate and wise man. She told him the whole story and her views. Mr. Harry asked her, "Why do you want to be a politician, Sarah?"

Sarah replied, "They are so powerful and make lots of money. I want power and money. Clearly this is the best career for me."

Mr. Harry smiled and replied, "Sarah you are being short-sighted. You are only considering those things that you want now. Ten years from now these things will not matter much. But, a stable career would. Politicians don't have a stable career. Those who are lucky enough to win are powerful for some years. After that, most of them become nobody. Both Obama and Osama call themselves powerful political leaders. And many people agree with them. You see both can't be right. Moreover, the so-called powerful Osama took many years to carry out his cowardly act in New York City in 2001. And the most powerful Obama took many years to kill Osama. In early 2011, he chickened out thrice and cancelled three 'kill' missions before reluctantly agreeing in May, 2011 to bring Osama to justice. Even then he was clearly jumpy, like a cat on a hot tin roof, while the brave Navy Seals were risking their lives at the other corner of the world. Besides, politics is not a main career option. In a democracy, anyone can become a politician at any time. You can think about it when you are mature enough," Mr. Harry paused, took a deep breath, and then continued his passionate lecture.

"You must have read stories about magicians. Long, long ago, magicians used to be the most powerful persons. Everyone from the common people to the kings used to seek their advice. But have you heard of any magician now? They are almost extinct. About a few centuries back, priests used to be the most powerful men, more than the kings were. Same way we don't know how long politicians will last. Even now, very few politicians command respect. Possibly in two or three decades they may also become powerless if not extinct. Just think about the present status of the powerful politicians of 2000. Who would have imagined that Gaddafi, the king of kings would be found in a drain pipe and killed like a dog? Who would have ever believed that Saddam Hussein would be found in a hole on the ground? Who would have thought that superrich and powerful Hosni Mubarak would be brought to the Court on his sick bed? The world is slowly becoming truly democratic, and democracy does not require powerful politicians. In true democracy, power is vested in the people and politicians are people's servants. Not the other way round."

Sarah seemed to be at a complete loss for words as she tried to digest the mind-boggling facts. And she herself was aware of the sad fate of many other powerful past politicians. She expectantly stared at the school counselor.

Mr. Harris could judge that now the stubborn, ignorant teen was ready for advice. So, he counseled her, "On the other hand, money is here to stay forever. And everyone needs advice on how to manage money. A financial advisor is also powerful and rich. Moreover, this career line is secure and stable. You are good in mathematics. You told me you don't like accounts. But I have seen your results. You get good marks in it. You should play your strengths. If you can get good marks in accounts when you don't like it, imagine what wonders you will be able to do if you start liking it. Remember, you should have a future plan. Start thinking with reference to your future plan. Whatever I am saying will make sense when you will appreciate what you would like to be in 10-15 years from now."

Sarah understood and realized her mistake in time. Today, she is a very successful financial advisor. She is making big money by advising others how to make money. What's more, she got her wish. She is rich and powerful.

Give-and-Take Session

Like Sarah, Chuck Colson also wanted to be a very powerful man when he was young. He became President Nixon's special counsel and had his own office in the White House with all the perks and prestige of a powerful position. Unfortunately, he went from the pinnacle of political power to the humiliation of becoming a convicted criminal. After serving time in prison, he forged a new career as a respected author and speaker. Colson, the famous author of 'born again' and many other books, realized in his second innings the futility of power and the utility of humility.

All children pass through various stages of development as they grow up. Each child has a unique developmental time frame and pattern. But all children are in the midst of a significant physical and emotional growth phase. And even a fully grown teenager's brain cannot control impulses or understand cause and effect like a mature adult brain. The recent groundbreaking neuroscience research confirms that mature thinking (cognitive maturity) develops last, i.e., after physical and mental maturity for all children. Some researchers estimate that cognitive development continues until age 25 to 30. Mature thinking includes using good judgment, associating cause and effect, using moral intelligence, being able to control impulses and link current behavior with future outcomes, and other thought processes associated with rational and responsible behavior.

Recently neuroscientist Daniel Levitin confirmed that 'Bieber Fever' is not only real, but it's a part of growing up. Using an MRI, Levitin found hearing familiar, favorite music – such as Justin Bieber's song – triggers a release of dopamine in the brain, which produces a pleasurable feeling. Hearing Justin Bieber's voice affects the pleasure and reward centers of the brain similar to the rush that comes with eating chocolate or winning a lottery.

Neuroscientists assert that during teenage years, the brain's frontal lobe (prefrontal cortex) grows considerably, causing its powers of reasoning and risk assessment to go askew. The frontal lobe is often referred to as the 'CEO of the brain'. It is responsible for regulating behavior, abstract thinking and thought analysis. When a specific part of the brain is still under construction, a teenager's brain doesn't work the same way as an adult's.

That's why it's not abnormal for children to make wrong choices. They don't do it intentionally. They can't make out the difference between right and wrong. But it is important to know that difference to achieve something in life. And the solution is to learn how to distinguish between the right and the wrong. Fortunately, children can always seek advice from their parents, teachers and other adult well-wishers.

Points to Ponder

- What is the purpose of a career pop quiz?
- Do you think career quizzes can help you choose the right career? Why?
- What is more important, money or happiness?
- Why Sarah wanted to become a politician?
- Why it is important to choose your career intelligently?
- In democracy, power is vested in the people and politicians are people's servants. It is true in theory but not in practice. What do you think?
- How many people do you know who really enjoy their career? What do they like or dislike about their job?
- What factors would you like to consider while choosing a career?
- What kinds of jobs interest you? What makes them interesting to you?
- You should play your strengths. What does it mean to you?

- What are your strengths and limitations? How would these strengths and limitations affect you in the jobs that interest you?
- Power corrupts and absolute power corrupts absolutely. Do you agree? Can you prove it wrong by giving three examples of political leaders?

The first step in your career journey is to know your strengths, talents and skills. We think we know a lot about ourselves and that may be true, but sometimes a little confirmation can help a lot. It is important to clearly know your skills, talents and real strengths. Remember it's a real strength to know your strengths. Appreciating your real strengths will help you maximize your potential and get closer to achieving your goals and dreams. It will also make you aware of the things you should and shouldn't do so that you can avoid costly career mistakes.

Children are most impressionable before the age of 18. And they can be easily influenced and convinced by what they see happening in the society. They have a tendency to follow all that is considered cool without a second thought. Unfortunately in most cases, the media is their teacher. And in this day and age of internet, the media is making the most of it. But then, there are many intelligent students who benefit from the wise people around them.

Are you listening to the wise people in your life? Do you take advantage of their advice?

May God bless you and guide you. I wish you the best!

4. The Story of Sir Tory

Purpose of the Module: This module deals with caring for the elderly so as to encourage children to be kind, considerate and compassionate towards the elderly people. Here the focus is less on the 'caring for elderly' in general and more on the caring for grandparents and other elderly relatives. The objective is to encourage impressionable children to create caring culture in their home first.

Key Values: Caring for Elders, Gratitude.
Supplementary Values: Reverence for Old Age, Duty.
Life Skills: Tolerance, Respect for Elders, Flexibility.
Estimated Storytelling Time: 5 to 7 Minutes
Give-and-Take Session: 5 to 9 Minutes

Tory was very sad because his wife Angelina died yesterday. He was heartbroken. The old man was feeling really lonely in Paris. His son, Tory Jr. lived in Chicago with his wife and a daughter.

Angelina was very fond of Paris. They came here five years ago when he retired from Orange, Inc. After retirement, he wanted a job so as to pay back the education loan he had taken for his son's engineering education. Fortunately, he got a good job as a school counselor in Paris, and hence Tory became Sir Tory.

Tory's son, Tory Jr. tried to convince him that he should retire now. And he should shift to Chicago and live with him. Tory told him that some installments of the loan were still unpaid. Tory Jr. suggested that he should pay the balance loan from his retirement kitty. After much persuasion, Tory agreed. He was very fond of his little granddaughter Sarah. He was happy as he was going to stay with her. He paid the loan from his retirement kitty and shifted to Chicago to live with his son.

Tory was experiencing depression due to the death of his beloved wife. His health also began to fail, as he was not leading an active life. Soon it became difficult for him to walk properly. So his son bought him a simple wood cane to walk.

Tory used to walk in the house using the cane. But his daughter-in-law was not happy with the marks that the stick left on the carpet. Soon he was restricted to his room only. His health further deteriorated. His hands began to shake and as a result, he would often drop his spectacles. Tory Jr. got them repaired every time instead of buying a new one. Sometimes he used to take weeks to get them repaired. As a result, Tory, who was an avid reader, could not even read books and newspapers. Sometimes he would spill his tonic, coffee, etc. on the carpet. His son and daughter-in-law were fed up with all the mess and told him to remain in his room all-day and eat there itself. He felt very lonely as he was not allowed to walk in the house. The old man was hurt by the treatment he was getting. But for Sarah, he would have committed suicide. He eagerly waited for Sarah's holidays when she played with him. Those were the only happy days for him.

One day, Tory Jr. saw his daughter was making something out of wood. When he enquired about it, the little girl thoughtfully replied, "Daddy, I am making a special stick for you and momma so that when you get old you can roam freely. I am trying to make such a stick that will not leave marks on the carpet, and so I won't have to limit your movement. And daddy I have decided that when I grow up. I will become an engineer and invent unbreakable glasses for you so that you can read whenever you want. Then you won't have to wait like grand-father does when you get his glasses repaired."

Tory Jr. was shocked to hear such words of wisdom from the little girl who was not even aware that good quality fiber sticks and unbreakable plastic lenses were already available in the market. This shock made Tory Jr. and his wife come to their senses. They realized their mistake. They thought better late than never.

With tears in their eyes, they went to the Tory's room and

apologized. Next day, Tory Jr. brought a light fiber stick and two pairs of good quality plastic specs for Tory. The family started eating together and spending time together. Tory's movement was no longer restricted. The happy atmosphere and little exercise had such an impact on the old man's health that within two weeks he could walk without the stick. His overall health also improved greatly, and he would no longer break or spill anything.

Love is the best therapy, which made Tory a healthy and happy man once again. True love truly heals.

Give-and-Take Session

Grandparents and grandchildren represent a grand love affair between the generations. This blind love affair between two even or odd generations is unique and universal. Grandparents are a wonderful blend of laughter, caring deeds, wonderful stories and love. They make the world of their grandchildren better than they could ever have dreamed.

Most of you have the chance to make a world of difference in your grandparents' lives. If you don't have this opportunity, you can always adopt a grandparent with the consent of your parents and spend some quality time together. This way you can show the seniors in our community that how special they are to us. And in the process you will also learn a lot from their wisdom.

In old age, people begin to feel lonely. Many research studies confirm that loneliness hurts us and connection heals us. Old age is the hardest part of the life's journey. It is our duty to make this part of the life of our old relatives as comfortable as we can. We should show them that they are most wanted and loved, and their advice and guidance is important for us.

Points to Ponder

- Why Tory Jr. asked his father to pay back the education loan from his retirement kitty?

- Do you think Tory Jr. himself should have paid the education loan taken for his engineering education?
- When Tory Jr. and Sarah were kids, they used to spoil clothes, carpet, etc. But their parents never stopped their movements. Do you think it was right on the part of Tory Jr. to stop his old father's movement in the house?
- Why do some people think old people are like old things, which have little or no value?
- Often grandparents become very happy when they see their grandchildren. What else can you do to make them really happy?
- Think a while about your grandparents and their needs. What you can do to show that you care for them?
- What steps would you suggest to ensure that people care for their aged parents?
- What do you think people want in their old age?

Your future is based on your present actions. You can contribute to create a caring culture in your home and society. You can show your love for your grandparents or other elderly relatives by:
- ✓ Spending time with them
- ✓ Listening to their advice
- ✓ Giving them flowers or personal cards on special days or whenever possible
- ✓ Greeting them on their birthday and other festivals
- ✓ Shifting some of your social networking time to family networking time
- ✓ Taking good care of yourself and your studies. Remember, your grandparents won't be happy if you are not taking good care of yourself
- ✓ Taking a trip with your grandparents. Special trips, whether it's a day trip to a nearby park, a weekend in a nearby city, or a week-long resort vacation, will always be remembered by your grandma and grandpa
- ✓ Keeping in mind that smart children can find smart ways to make their near and dear ones happy.

We should be caring, considerate and compassionate towards our grandparents. And we should always remember that they need our love. Remember, the love of a family is life's greatest blessing.

A beautiful quote from Harry Emerson Fosdick summarizes the power of love "Bitterness imprisons life; love releases it. Bitterness paralyzes life; love empowers it. Bitterness sours life; love sweetens it. Bitterness sickens life; love heals it. Bitterness blinds life; love anoints its eyes."

5. An Echo from the Past

Purpose of the Module: The objective is to make children aware about the strength and unconditional nature of a mother's love. Equally important is to remind them about selfless, boundless love of parents for their children who often take them for granted and show no respect or appreciation for their efforts, and sometimes even act rude towards their parents.

Key Values: Responsibility to Parents, Unconditional Love.
Supplementary Values: Gratitude, Tolerance, Humanism.
Life Skills: Good Habits, Flexibility, Balance.
Estimated Storytelling Time: 5 to 8 Minutes
Give-and-Take Session: 6 to 11 Minutes

For as long as he could remember, Stan hated his mother. His mom had only one hand, and the left side of her face was badly scarred and distorted. She worked at a railway station to bring him up. Stan always considered her an embarrassment.

When he was in the elementary school, his mom came to his school on the occasion of mother's day. Everyone who saw her gave him a look of pity before returning their gaze towards her. He was so embarrassed. Stan hated being pitied upon. He felt very bad, but he knew there was nothing he could do, except curse his mom in his heart for being the cause of his suffering.

Next day his classmates taunted him for his mother's appearance and a missing hand. They asked him the reason. He told them that he didn't know. This was the truth. He never felt like asking her the reason. Whatever maybe the reason she was a shame for him.

Stan hated her so much that sometimes he wondered how great his life would be if she had died earlier.

Whenever children taunted him, he cursed her to die. His mom knew that he wished she died because sometimes he used to say it on her face. She never said anything about it to him. He knew she couldn't say anything because even she knew what a shame she was.

Stan was desperate to run from this pathetic life. He decided to study hard and get admission into a good college. Few years later, his dream came true. He got admission into a good university. He left his home and vowed never to return.

Stan completed his degree and got a good job. He got married and was blessed with a son. He really loved his little son. All was well.

One day he got the shock of his life. His mother came to his house from nowhere. He hadn't been in touch with her for years. In fact, he never thought about her since he left for college years ago. He didn't even invite her on his wedding knowing that it would only embarrass him. When his little son saw her, he started crying and hid under the table.

Stan told his mother, "Can't you see my happiness? Have you come here to ruin it? Just go back and let me live in peace," he shouted angrily. "I don't want to see your face ever again."

Lovingly and longingly staring at her grandson whom she had come to meet, Stan's mother replied, "I am sorry. It seems I lost my way because of my poor memory."

Stan never heard from her after that. He was relieved. His life revolved around his beloved son. One day his aunt, his mother's sister, wrote him a letter informing that his mother had died. The news had no impact on him. He was not going to attend her funeral.

In the evening, when Stan's son came back from the college, he saw the letter. He enquired about his grandma. Stan narrated him the case of her last visit. While Stan exaggerated the incident, his son blamed him for the petty treatment given to his grandma. He told Stan that he should have handled his innocent son instead of throwing his mother out. He was very sad. Next day, he went on a college trip.

In fact, Stan's son had gone to attend his grandma's funeral. There his grandma's sister told him the whole story, including the accident in which his grandma lost her hand.

When Stan was two years old, his left feet got stuck in the railway track while crossing it. Stan's mother tried hard to free his leg, but it was badly stuck. When she saw the train was coming, she tried to put her hand under his feet with all the force she could manage. She didn't stop even when she fractured her hand in the rescue operation. She prayed to God to save her son's feet and take her hand instead. Just in the nick of time, she got some amazing power and she could insert her hand under Stan's feet, and Stan was freed from the metal death trap. But unfortunately her hand was cut and face was badly burnt by the train. The railway company praised her outstanding courage and sacrifice, and offered her a job in the organization.

After a fortnight, Stan received a last letter from his son. There was just one sentence in the letter, which said, "I don't want to see your face ever again."

After that, Stan never heard from his son. But in the last ten years, all that he heard was: "I don't want to see your face ever again."

A very sad and lonely Stan often wondered whether these were the last words of his son or the echo of his last words to his mother.

Give-and-Take Session

Few years ago, when the author narrated Stan's story to some children to test its moral potential, it was liked by most children, and it scored well on the moral quotient and impact scale. But many children were not convinced that such a thing could happen in real life. The author was more than happy to see that the children were creatively criticizing the tale. It showed that the message has hit home.

Here also some children were of the view that the sacrifice of Stan's mother was an abnormal case. It was not an abnormal case. Given a chance most mothers would do the same thing. There are many similar real life examples which demonstrate what a mother's love truly means, how it knows no bounds, no limits. When a mother has the chance to protect and empower her child, she will do whatever it takes.

Here is a comparable true life story. Recently a woman in Indiana lost part of both of her legs as she shielded her children from two tornadoes that slammed into their home.

Stephanie Decker was at home when her husband texted her that a tornado was moving directly towards their three-story home in Indiana. She picked up her children, eight-year-old Dominic and five-year-old Reese, from school earlier than usual when she heard the storm was approaching.

Just minutes before the tornado swept through, Decker took her young son and daughter to the basement. To protect them, she covered them with a blanket and threw herself on top of them to shield them from debris.

In no time, everything started hitting her. She was holding them and trying to keep everything away from them to protect them. Pillars, beams, furniture, everything was just slamming into her back, but she continued to protect her children who were very scared and crying. She was no match for the catastrophe but she did not relent. She stood guard. Selflessness is the thing that makes a mother far braver than the bravest, and tough in a way that seems to contradict her femininity.

After a while, a neighbor came to her rescue. Realizing the severity of Stephanie's injuries, he ran for help and found a Deputy Sheriff traveling on an all-terrain vehicle about a quarter of a mile away. Soon enough, the deputy applied compression bandages to Stephanie Decker's legs to halt her blood loss.

Her children emerged from the storm completely unharmed but the wreckage broke seven of her ribs and almost completely severed both of her legs.

Points to Ponder
(It is not necessary for students to answer the questions or participate in discussion. They are just required to ponder over them. So, after every question or statement, a brief pause is recommended so as to allow their subconscious mind to absorb the desired values.)

- Why Stan hated his mother?
- Why Stan's mother didn't tell him about the accident? Do you think she didn't want him to feel guilty about it?
- Stan's mother really loved him, but Stan left her? Why?
- Stan really loved his son, but he left Stan? Why?
- God created mothers because He wanted to show Himself to little children through them. Do you agree?
- How do you show gratitude and honor your mother? Do you reciprocate your mother's love and caring?
- If your mother often scolds you, does it mean she doesn't love you?
- What does it take to make your mother happy?

There is no other love like a mother's love for her children. Mothers love you unconditionally. Mothers love you when you are sad. They love you even if you are bad. Mothers are nurturing, protective, and instinctive in caring for their children; it is universal.

There is nothing like a mother's love, and mothers from the animal kingdom are no exception. Nearly all animals are good mothers. God has not given animals a good brain. But God has given good maternal instincts to most animal mothers. There are plenty of species in the animal kingdom who make better mothers than humans. But then, while most of us have to work hard at raising the children, lots of animals don't bother to parent their young at all.

As is the case with most things in life, here also we can expect exceptions. There are great mothers, and there are not so great mothers. God's production line is not mechanical, or computerized.

And God loves variety. All animals, including humans are god-made creations. While most mothers are good mothers, some chose to ignore their maternal instincts. While such unusual mothers from animal kingdom have their survival reasons, such weird human mothers just ignore God-given maternal instincts for materialistic reasons.

There is a recent case of a Japanese mother who was accused of parental neglect of her 1-year-old son who died of pneumonia while she was chatting on the Internet. Otsu Police said she failed to seek medical treatment for her son, didn't change his diapers and left him unattended on a bed in their apartment until the boy succumbed to pneumonia. The 29-year-old mother was aware that her toddler was feverish, yet she did not attend him for days. Perhaps God wanted us all to see the difference between a mother and a so-called mother. Then again, it is said that during Japan's earthquake of March 2011, a mother endured a big injury to her body as she used her own body to protect her baby, and finally she sacrificed her own life to save her child.

Whether your mother is great or good, you should try to become a great child. Remember, there is no greater love than that between a mother and her child. Nothing can reciprocate your mother's love, care, and concern, but you should express something as a token of appreciation of what she has done for you. It's time to let your mother know that you really appreciate her.

6. The Perils of Plagiarism

Purpose of the Module: This section is designed to familiarize students with the perils of plagiarism and how this seemingly innocent habit can affect their career in the long term. Students should also be discouraged to use sms type short words and twitter type sentences in their academic writings.

Key Values: Integrity, Quest for knowledge.
Supplementary Values: Avoiding Plagiarism, Truthfulness, Kindness to Animals.
Life Skills: Writing Skills, Hard Work, Self-help.
Estimated Storytelling Time: 5 to 8 Minutes
Give-and-Take Session: 6 to 9 Minutes

The English teacher Miss Bella was worried. Her students often copied their assignments from the internet and submitted as their own work. This worried her greatly, as they were not learning anything.

What's more, many students were frequently using SMS lingo or twitter type slang words and abbreviations in their school work. With excessive use of social networking sites, they were forgetting the right spelling of simple words, and their sentence structure seemed to be hurried and a bit choppy. Sometimes their assignments looked as if they were based on the grammar of an alien planet.

To find out a workable solution, she discussed her problem with the science teacher Miss Jessica who was considered the wisest teacher of the school. Miss Bella rued that irresponsible use of technology was spoiling the well-established, centuries old principles of language. She blamed the parents who were too busy with their work to care what was going on in the lives of their children.

The science teacher, however, didn't consider shortening the words and simplifying the sentences as a serious issue because she felt language should not be rigid or watertight; language should evolve over time. But, she viewed plagiarism as a real threat to the academic world. Miss Jessica also agreed that students weren't at fault. They were merely imitating others. In fact, when most celebrities and leaders, including the president Obama and the slain terrorist Osama, were using shortened language, how could we blame the impressionable children? She agreed that parents were responsible for neglecting their children and their habits. Miss Jessica advised her to go to the local pastor and seek his guidance since the problem looked serious and, as such, would require divine intervention. Miss Bella agreed and decided to meet the pastor soon.

Next Saturday, Miss Bella went to the pastor's home. When he opened the door to let her in, his small kitten, Emily ran out of the door. Emily started running and playing in the garden. The pastor got worried as Emily could harm herself if she went outside on the road. He tried hard to call Emily inside but the happy cat was busy playing. Then the pastor went inside and got Emily's food bowl. He kept the empty food bowl just inside the door. Seeing the food bowl, the innocent kitten came running and once she was inside, the pastor closed the door. Miss Bella was watching all this with amusement

When the pastor politely asked Miss Bella what he could do for her, she replied that she just felt like meeting him. So, she just came to pay her respects. They chatted about the cats and their life. While observing the little cat's facial expressions, Miss Bella remarked, "It's amazing how cats can forget and forgive what humans do to them. Cats know how to live in the present moment; they do not tend to worry about the past or future."

The pastor replied, "All animals know how to live in the present, unlike humans, who constantly live in the past or the future, worrying excessively about other people or their wealth. While giving reasoning and thinking abilities to humans, God expected a responsible behavior from humans. And we think animals don't think, but really, we cannot say that for sure. All we can be sure of is that animals know how to live a worry free life. God intentionally made animals different from humans who excessively worry about the future they imagine, grumble about the past they recall, and worry about what others did, thought, or might do."

While giving a milk chocolate to the lovely cat, Miss Bella commented how animals could teach us a lot about living peaceful, joyful, mindful lives. After some time, Miss Bella left.

On Monday when Miss Jessica enquired her about whether she got the solution to her problem or not, Miss Bella told her the cat story. She then said, "I didn't feel like asking the pastor as he himself was not very honest with his pet?"

She continued, "However, I got my solution by watching that interesting scene. I just have to give some sort of incentive to my students so that they work hard and avoid SMS lingo or abbreviations in their school work. I will make them realize the importance of English in their career and life. When they will understand the future benefits they will derive from a good command over the language, they will avoid short text versions and seriously do their assignments on their own. Moreover, I will start giving bonus marks and better grades to the original assignments. This will encourage students to work on their own and develop their language skills further."

Miss Jessica added, "You are right. We should teach them the difference between texting lingo and correct English. And I believe they can separate the way they write their academic writings and text-messages. It isn't that our children can't decipher the difference of when to use shorthand. It's just that they haven't been taught when and where to use it. We, teachers get so caught up in saying that a student's work is 'right' or 'wrong' that we forget to explain the rationale."

Miss Bella smiled and quipped, "Once again you proved that

students are not at fault."

Give-and-Take Session

In this day and age, you can find absolutely everything on the Internet, making plagiarism easier than ever. All students are not strong enough. Some are vulnerable and take the easy way out. They are often tempted to use others' words in their writing assignments. It is very important for the students to understand what constitutes plagiarism because it is a serious breach of academic integrity.

Plagiarism is the act of taking another person's writing, conversation, poem, or even idea and passing it off as your own. It's a form of cheating because it's stealing another person's ideas. It's not allowed in schools, colleges, or beyond. And it's always better to learn the right way to use information resources, such as websites, books, and magazines. You can make good use of the resources as well as avoid plagiarizing by following these guidelines.

- ✓ Cite the source of all ideas, opinions, facts, and statistics that are not common knowledge. You don't have to cite if the information is common knowledge and is not considered the work of any particular person.
- ✓ Never copy and paste unless you intend to use a direct quotation.
- ✓ Give the author of the material credit by 'citing' your source.
- ✓ You can use information and facts, but avoid copying others' original interpretation or research based on those facts.
- ✓ Give credit whenever you use a direct quote by placing it in quotation marks.
- ✓ Give credit to the author or authors whenever you paraphrase (express the same message in different words) a thought, idea, or sentence.

Points to Ponder

- • Why Miss Bella was worried about students' future?

- The English teacher was worried about students using SMS type slang words and abbreviations in their writings. But the science teacher didn't consider it a very serious issue. What are your views?
- When the pastor lured the cat with an empty food bowl, do you think he was not honest with his pet?
- Do you think the pastor's act was right as it was for the safety and wellbeing of the cat?
- Do you think it was an act of dishonesty on the part of Miss Bella when she lied to the pastor about the purpose of her visit? Why?
- When you cheat or plagiarize, you are cheating yourself as well as cheating other honest students. Do you agree?
- Not all lies are bad. All people lie sometimes, and it is okay to lie sometimes. What do you think?
- Do you hate your parents for lying to you about Santa Claus? (Of course not!) Do you hate them for telling you the truth about Santa? (Of course not!)
- Why animals are different from humans who worry about the future they imagine, grumble about the past they recall, and worry about what others did, thought, or might do?
- Would you favor the ultimate truth even if it's a bad thing to say?
- It is said that when helping the wounded, honesty is secondary to healing. What are your views?

Honesty is more than just not telling lies. Not telling the truth also means dishonesty. Not telling the truth may take many forms, and may lead to many consequences. Not clearly mentioning your sources is academically dishonest and may lead to charges of plagiarism. This is a sort of stealing and cheating. It isn't just morally wrong but also illegal.

Integrity demands that we should not steal or cheat. Stealing means taking anything that doesn't belong to us without asking its owner. Cheating means we are not playing by the rules. To cheat in a game is not to cheat referees or umpires, but it is to cheat the other players. And when you cheat in the school, you are not cheating the teachers. You are cheating yourself of an education as well as cheating other students who play by the rules. It demoralizes other students and affects the mutual trust between students. Remember, the teachers always prefer an honest, even if imperfect, effort from their students rather than the perfect work of someone else.

It doesn't feel good when people lie to us, take our things, or play unfairly. If we want others to be honest with us, we must be honest too.

7. A Trip to the Zoo

Purpose of the Module: This section is designed to remind the students about the importance of healthy habits and living a healthy lifestyle. Healthy habits such as proper nutrition and exercise are crucial to a child's development as well as success in life. The idea is to get them thinking about how both humans and nature need to live in balance to be happy and healthy.

Key Values: Healthy Eating, Positive Thinking.
Supplementary Values: Healthy Living, Willpower, Kindness to Animals.
Life Skills: Thinking Skills, Good Habits, Self-control.
Estimated Storytelling Time: 5 to 8 Minutes
Give-and-Take Session: 6 to 10 Minutes

The class was going on a field trip to the zoo. All the students were very excited about the trip. After all, they were going to see the wonderful display of animals in their natural settings.

Before entering the zoo, Miss Minerva told the students that they were going to see so many creatures. And creating so many species of animals involved the highest form of magic. We could not even imagine the powers of that magician. After all the technological advances, we could not even create a single fly on our own.

Miss Minerva also told the class that it was not just a fun trip, but also meant to assess their observation skills. And they were supposed to record their observations based on which she would be grading them. Students' observations should relate to the animal's life style, for example, their habits, behavior patterns, etc. Whatever they observe, they must pen it down.

Just after entering the zoo, Miss Minerva herded all the students in one corner and counted them like sheep. Then she instructed, "Everyone should be kind to the animals and behave responsibly. Remember, to err is human, but to forgive is not my policy."

All the students were very excited about the opportunity to discover and learn together in a fun way. They roamed in the zoo for about two hours, after which everyone assembled at the food court to have lunch. All the little boys and girls were very happy, and they were busy telling each other what they saw. After lunch, they went back to the school.

Later in the class, Miss Minerva briefed the students about the zoo trip. She then asked students to stand up one at a time in front of the class and share with other students their observations.

Little Lee came and said, "Meerkats keep a lookout on their surroundings. They are in their cages and protected from predators but they keep a lookout as this behavior is inherent to them and they cannot get rid of it."

Miss Minerva smiled and announced, "Very good, Lee. You get an A."

Then Crabbe said, "I saw that parrots are of many colors."

Everyone laughed. Miss Minerva commented, "Think more Crabbe and come back with something new and interesting after others complete their chance."

After that Hermione came forward and said, "I observed that almost all animals looked happier, healthier and more content than human beings. It is because of their natural lifestyle. They were eating only natural, appropriate foods and living a natural life even in the man-made environment. They follow a healthy lifestyle and appropriate diet. They don't indulge in junk foods, sugary snacks and soft drinks."

Miss Minerva said, "Very good Hermione. That's a great observation. You gave a very good reply. You get an A+."

Then Draco came and said, "I saw that the baby elephant was tied with a very heavy iron chain to an iron pillar whereas the big elephant was tied using a simple nylon rope to a small wooden stake. This is just my observations. I cannot tell why it is so."

"Very good observation, Draco. You get an A," Miss Minerva smiled and posed a question. "Now I would like all of you to think and tell me the reason behind this."

Hoping to get a better grade or at least finish his turn, Crabbe answered, "It is because the baby elephant does not know the way. If it gets lost, it won't be able to come back whereas the older elephant can come back."

"Good try Crabbe. But it is not correct. As I said before, I never repeat myself. Think more and give a well-reasoned reply," Miss Minerva said. Looking at poker-faced Crabbe, she quipped, "O.K. Here is another one for you. If you try to fail, and you succeed, which one have you done? Think about it and tell me after the class."

Then George came and said, "It's because the zookeeper must have made a mistake. He must have swapped the rope with chain and tied the baby elephant to the iron pillar meant for the older elephant."

Miss Minerva said, "The answer is not right but still it is funny. You get a B for trying George. Anyone else would like to try?"

After that there was a pin drop silence in the class, and all the students were scratching their heads for an answer.

Then Hermione stepped forward again and confidently said, "In captivity, baby elephants are trained not to roam. To condition a baby elephant not to stray, its one leg is tied with a chain. Initially the baby elephant tries to break free from the chain, but the chain is too strong. After many futile attempts, the baby elephant 'learns' that it can't break the chain. And this leaves a permanent impression on its mind. When the elephant grows up and becomes strong, it could easily break the chain. But because it 'learned' that it couldn't break the chain when it was young, the big elephant thinks that it still can't break the rope, so it doesn't even try. It learns to live in a state called 'learned helplessness'. That is why the baby elephant is tied to an iron pillar with heavy metal chains that cannot be broken easily. And the big elephant is tied with a simple rope even though it is much stronger and bigger than the baby elephant."

The class was listening with rapt attention. Miss Minerva announced, "Good thinking Hermione! You gave the correct explanation. You have already got an A+ for demonstrating good observation skills. And now I declare you the champion of this class."

Everyone clapped for Hermione.

Give-and-Take Session

Every child is a unique blessing, a gift full of promise and potential. And every child deserves a future full of health and happiness; a future full of hope and possibilities.

In order to realize their full potential, children need to grow up in a loving, stimulating and nurturing environment. Such an environment helps children develop strong bodies and healthy attitudes that will strongly influence their health as adults.

Children need a healthy, balanced diet that gives them enough nutrients and energy to grow and develop. Accordingly, children should take in more energy than they use, and this extra energy forms new tissues as they grow. But, if children regularly take in too much energy, this is stored as fat and they will put on weight.

When children gain large amounts of weight they do add extra fat cells. These fat cells develop and multiply greatly during the childhood. Once we hit adulthood, we have all the fat cells we will ever have, and they get bigger or smaller depending on our energy intake. So, childhood is the time to control weight problems later in life. Remember, childhood is the time to acquire healthy eating habits.

We all know that having a calcium-rich diet during childhood and teenage makes a big difference in health, now and later. Bones rely on calcium they store during childhood to stay strong throughout life. So, childhood is the time to build up bones as much as possible.

And it is not just the case of calcium. Your body requires many nutrients, which you can get from a balanced, healthy diet. But nobody's perfect when it comes to healthful eating. When it comes to food, we are like animals. Most of us have some weaknesses. But we should always remember that it is difficult to get the nutrients we need if we are eating wrong types of foods.

Junk foods and colas contain empty calories, i.e., calories without any nutrients. Normally processed foods, fried foods, and sugary foods are the main culprits that lure you away from the path of healthy eating. Try to avoid these foods. While it is easier said than done but you don't have a choice if you want a good personality.

Points to Ponder

- What was the highest form of magic that Miss Minerva was referring?
- Who was the magician referred by Miss Minerva?
- Can you explain why God created so many kinds of animals? If God was really the creator why would he waste time creating so many species only for them to become extinct?
- Why did God create so many variations of the same species, for example, parrots of many colors and sizes?
- Why Crabbe's first observation was not considered by Miss Minerva?
- Like elephants, can we become victims of 'learned helplessness'?
- Do you have good observation skills? How you can further develop your observation skills?
- Childhood obesity has more than tripled in the past 30 years.

- Why is childhood obesity on the rise, and what can we do to prevent it?
- Why are more and more children showing signs of stress and mental illness?
- Why childhood is the best time to acquire good habits? Why childhood and teenage years are known as the formative years?
- What is the Creator's purpose in creating the universe?

Have you ever wondered why do humans take so long to reach adulthood? When compared to other animals, why do our children take so long to grow up?

First, we have a longer lifespan than most animals. Second, we take a long time to learn all the skills that make us a special species. We take more time to reach adulthood because of our unique developmental and learning requirements. Our children have to imbibe good habits, moral values, life skills, etc. to lead a successful life.

What's more, what we learn during the formative years tends to stick. The attitudes and behaviors which are implanted during the formative years make us who we are in later life. That is why the best way to develop healthy habits for life is to start early, and incorporate good habits into your daily routine. After a while, they become a second nature, and you will do them robotically, like breathing, you do it, you just don't notice that you are doing it.

Now is the time when you can have the most significant influence on your lifelong health and personality. Remember, you are the one who is in control of your destiny and fate. The choices you make today will influence your life forever!

8. The Winner's Way

Purpose of the Module: This story aims to encourage children to recognize their talents and develop them into strengths. They should be encouraged to make sensible and satisfying career choices. They should have confidence, winning attitude, and optimism to meet life's challenges head on and strive for success. While children are free to choose their hobbies, role models, etc., they should understand the consequences of their decisions.

Key Values: Quest for Knowledge, Perseverance, Abstinence
Supplementary Values: Duty, Self-discipline, Forward Looking, Willpower
Life Skills: Hard Work, Creative Thinking, Initiative, Devotion
Estimated Storytelling Time: 5 to 8 Minutes
Give-and-Take Session: 5 to 9 Minutes

Paul wanted to be a game developer for PlayStation. Earlier he used to enjoy playing computer games, but now all he wanted was to make computer games. He realized that while playing games was an unproductive pastime, making games involved learning a rewarding skill. Paul was good at animation and C++, the preferred language to write games software. He wanted to achieve something big in life, and he knew that all achievers like Bill Gates, Steve Jobs, Richard Branson, Michael Dell, Mark Zuckerberg and Warren Buffet started early in life to chase their dreams.

But he required a PlayStation and a powerful Computer to start his programming practice. Paul began saving money by reducing his phone bills. He also started going to school on bicycle instead of taking bus. Despite his best efforts, his savings were not enough to buy the required devices in the near future. He was a bit disturbed, wondering what he could do about it.

His friend Gaga suggested that he could work part time in her aunt's office to gain some experience as well as earn money. Paul gladly accepted the offer to work with Mrs. Seth after school hours.

Mrs. Seth recognized the talent in Paul. She helped him to further improve his programming skills. Paul was happy to get such an opportunity. So, he dedicated his heart and mind to the work.

His friends would often ask him, "Why don't you join us today for a movie? Or we are going to the PlayMall, would you like to come?"

Whenever his friends asked him such questions, he always replied, "I am sorry guys. I can't come." Paul also wanted to enjoy, but not at the cost of his goal. He knew that this was the time to achieve something in life. And there would be ample opportunities to enjoy life.

After six months, Paul approached Mrs. Seth and said, "Ma'am, I think I have saved enough money to buy that old game development set which no one uses in the office. Can I buy that spare set?

Mrs. Seth asked, "How much have you saved?"

Paul stated the amount. Mrs. Seth replied sympathetically, "I'm sorry my child but I can't give you that old game set."

Paul was disheartened, wondering how he would take part in the design contest scheduled after two months. Somehow, he managed a weak smile and blurted, "It's ok Mrs. Seth. I just wanted to practice and enter the State Game Design Competition."

Mrs. Seth replied, "I think you can get a much better game development unit with your money. I was thinking of buying myself a new game set and I think you can buy my personal set."

Paul was stunned. Mrs. Seth's game development set was very advanced and expensive. He never even dreamed of owning such an advanced computer and that too so soon.

As he was digesting this bit of information, Mrs. Seth told him to take the machines whenever he wanted. With a lump in his throat, he thanked her and paid her the money.

Paul had two months to prepare for the game design competition. He worked hard on his new computer and took part in the competition. The game he submitted had entertainment as well as learning elements aimed at promoting creative and analytical skills of children.

He won the first prize. He not only got a commendation certificate but also a cash award, which was enough to fund a professional game development course at a good college. What's more, Great Apple Inc. signed him for a $10 million contract to develop a similar game for the iPad and iPhone platforms.

Paul became the hero of the state. His family and friends were very excited. While congratulating him, his friends said, "While all of us were busy having fun, you were working hard. You have the commitment, aspiration, and self-control required to succeed. What a difference you've made to your life. Congrats!"

Paul smiled and replied, "Thanks. My mission is over. Now I'm always ready to join you on fun trips."

Give-and-Take Session

Champions and achievers like Bill Gates, Steve Jobs and Paul have one thing in common. They know how to control their thoughts. Negative events and circumstances don't deter them. They know the events and circumstances are neutral. Our opinions about them are not.

We all have our own way of seeing the world. An ordinary person blames his environment or those around him for his problems and frustrations. But a winner uses negatives or criticism to be a better person; he uses his positives to the best of his abilities. He knows that life keeps on changing and no situation ever remains the same.

A winner focuses on the future.

When we don't learn how to control our mind, then we become a slave to circumstances, emotions, and other people's opinions. And when we intentionally nurture positive, focused thoughts, our circumstances steer us in a positive direction.

When we expect good things to happen, we are more likely to get good results. When we 'expect good' we are invoking the 'law of attraction' to work for us and bring to us what we expect. When we expect good things, our whole psyche is at work to attract the things which really matter to us, and avoid the things which we don't want in our lives.

When we know what we want to accomplish, and our emotions fully support it, then life brings us what we want. When we have a dream and the required passion to realize it, our positive energies come together to make it happen. And then our negative energies have little role to play in our life.

Points to Ponder

- Why Paul wanted to become a game developer? Why he shifted his interest from playing computer games to making computer games?
- Paul started going to school on bicycle instead of taking bus. Was he trying to reduce his carbon footprints?
- Paul was not even a qualified programmer. Why Great Apple Inc. signed him for a $10 million contract?
- Our fate is created by our own actions. What do you think?
- The life we experience is nourished by the thoughts we think. What we experience presently, both good and bad, is determined by our thoughts and actions in the past. Do you agree?
- How we take things in life matters a lot. Failures are just milestones on the road to success, often taking us closer to success. Do you agree?
- Childhood is the time to enjoy life and remain carefree. What is your opinion about it?

- Our thoughts are influenced by the way we were born and brought up and by our environment. Do you agree?
- What would you like to follow – your ambition or your passion?

The ancient texts known as the Upanishads declare, "You are what your deep, driving desire is. As your desire is, so is your will. As your will is, so is your deed. As your deed is, so is your destiny."

Our desires dictate our choices, and our choices determine our actions. The desires we act on decide our fate. By being responsible for our desires, we begin to create a world that truly reflects our dreams and desires.

We decide our own destiny. Our success or failure is up to us. Everything in life responds positively to our positive thoughts and actions.

Our positive or negative thoughts prompt what we say, what we do. The idea that 'we are what we think' is not a new one.

In fact, our thoughts prompt our acts and our acts direct our destiny. By taking control of our thoughts, we can control our world, our life.

Because humans are thinking beings, like fish are swimming beings and flowers are flowering beings, we have a tendency to think the whole time we are awake. We think between 40,000 and 60,000 thoughts per day. Most of those thoughts are the same ones from the past and negative. Every moment we have a choice – to be at peace or to be in resistance. It's a simple choice and yet many of us impulsively choose to live in negativity.

Don't cheat yourself. Don't compromise yourself and consequently compromise your life's goals. When negativity stares at you, it is time to say no. Every time you find yourself worrying, or being negative, just say no. Say no to negatives... say no to fears... say no to difficulties... say no to failures. Clear the negative thoughts, and try to delete them forever.

And don't go after cheap thrills. Don't go after the frills. Acquire the skills that will help you fulfill your dreams. Nurture positive thoughts and dreams; dreams that will propel you to reach your ambitions and aspirations. Positive thinking is a mental attitude; it is a way of seeing life. Embrace the positive thinking and set your ambition based on your passion. Your life will blossom and be just as wonderful as any beautiful garden you may imagine.

Remember, this is the right age to follow your ambition and your passion. And your ambition should have passion, and your passion should have ambition.

9. The Cause of The Pause

Purpose of the Module: This section is designed to make students aware that friendship is a give and take relationship, and there are responsibilities or expectations associated with friendship. Students should appreciate that they have the responsibility to be a good, dependable friend. They should realize that there is a mutuality of concern, caring, sharing and trust in friendship. And this mutuality creates a special bond that calls for special responsibilities.

Key Values: Friendship, Responsibility to Friends.
Supplementary Values: Respect for the Environment, Self-discipline, Team Spirit.
Life Skills: Good Manners, Team Work, Self-control.
Estimated Storytelling Time: 5 to 7 Minutes
Give-and-Take Session: 6 to 8 Minutes

'Teach the Teachers' was the theme of the vocational project. Miss Diana wanted students to apply their knowledge to make any project which could make our world a better place. Students were free to choose their partners. Students were also allowed to use information from the internet and library in addition to their knowledge.

Lily, Sarah and Emily, the three best friends formed their group and selected environment pollution as their topic. They decided to divide the project in 3 parts, namely, air pollution, water pollution and earth pollution. They agreed to write 5 pages each so as to ensure that their project report had at least 15 pages as required by Miss Diana. They also decided to establish that all the three categories of pollution often interacted with one another, with one type of pollution often spreading and leading to another form. They also wanted to show why it's important to control pollution and how this 'vicious cycle' could be converted to 'virtuous cycle' as was the case a few decades back.

Lily chose air pollution as it was the most important in view of the increasing vehicular pollution. Sarah and Emily took water pollution and earth pollution. The three best friends decided to coordinate and conclude their project after holidays in the school on the day of submission.

Sarah and Emily wrote a well-researched and hard-hitting report about water and earth pollution in six pages each. They were confident of getting a good grade.

On the day of submission, they asked Lily about her papers so that they could consolidate and conclude. Lily sheepishly replied that she didn't get time to work on the report, as she had to prepare for her science test. Her friends were shocked. Sarah asked in disbelief, "How could you ditch us like this? We were supposed to work together on it."

Lily calmly replied, "Chill guys. It's a group report. We will at least get a 'B' grade on it. Whereas in the science test, I am on my own and have to score well."

Sarah said, "If you didn't have time, why didn't you inform us?"

Lily casually replied, "I forgot to mention it. Don't make a fuss. We can always submit it later. Now let's discuss about holidays."

When the time to submit the project came, the teacher asked them why their project was not complete. All three friends looked down and didn't reply. It was a big pause. The teacher asked again, but they still replied with a pause. The teacher said that 15 pages was the minimum limit, and she was not going to accept their incomplete project. As a result, all three of them got a 'D' grade. While the 'D' grade for the studious girls was big news, other students were more curious about the cause of the pause.

Sarah and Emily were very angry with Lily. They stopped talking to her. Lily also felt bad at getting the 'D' grade and worse for losing her two friends for such a silly mistake.

A few days went by, and Lily got miserable without her friends. She realized that she had let her friends down and decided to apologize. She hoped that they would forgive her instead of forgetting her.

Next day she gathered courage and went to the front of the class and said, "Sarah, Emily I'm sorry. I know as a member of the group and being your friend, I should not have done that. Ma'am I ran away from my responsibility and acted selfishly. It was not their fault; they completed their assigned parts whereas I didn't. I'm really sorry."

The teacher smiled and said, "I hope you have learnt your lesson Lily. Don't repeat it in future. Children who really learn from their mistakes and are sincere about improvement never repeat the same mistakes. They gain from their mistakes and learn both responsibility and duty to others. They become strong and develop a strong sense of responsibility for their actions."

Sarah and Emily forgave lily. The three girls were best friends again. When the next group project came, Lily worked very hard to compensate for her earlier mistake, and the group got an 'A'.

Give-and-Take Session

Life is nothing without friendship. Having friends in our lives is very important. Study after study shows that having friends is one of the most important things we can do to stay healthy and happy.

It is said that a friend is a gift you give yourself. Friendship is indeed a true blessing. It doubles your joys, and divides your sorrows. Friendships can enrich our lives with memorable experiences and happy encounters.

Since the gift of friendship is given freely, many people take it for granted. They make unfair use of this gift and try to have it only for their benefit. A friendship made just to get some type of benefit is bound to fail miserably, with both sides being hurt.

In a friendship, you have certain rights but you also have responsibilities for your actions. And if your friendship is important to you, you should not take the responsibilities lightly that come along with it. Always remember, you have the responsibility to be a good friend to your friends, at least as good a friend as you wish them to be to you.

Do you know your responsibilities as a friend? Understanding the responsibilities of friendship can help you win true friends. Here are some tips and hints on how you can be a responsible friend.

- Be reliable and dependable; when you agree to do something, do it.
- Take responsibility for your actions; don't make excuses or blame others.
- Listen to your friends. You need to hear your friends' thoughts, feelings, and ideas. Everyone yearns for others' understanding. The best way to show your understanding is to listen.
- Try to think for friends, and be considerate of their troubles. Friends need to support one another's emotional needs. Try to help them win and be glad for their success.
- Forgive and forget. No one is perfect, and making mistakes is a normal part of life. We shouldn't constantly remind one another of past mistakes.
- Don't let your bad emotion influence your friendship. The words spoken out when you are angry can ruin your friendship. Also remember, it's not always what you say, often it's how you say it. Use your head; think before you act; imagine the consequences.
- Take care of your own business. Don't make others do what you are supposed to do.
- Be humble and avoid being judgmental. Friends often have different desires, opinions, and ideas. They have the right to think differently. We need to respect each others' unique points of view.
- Always treat your friends as you would like them to treat you.

Friendship is a give and take relationship. It's not one-sided. While being friends with someone means sharing responsibilities, it does not mean that friendship is a 'barter' business. But then again, your friend should not feel that he or she is always shouldering the responsibilities.

Points to Ponder

- Can we control pollution and convert the 'vicious cycle' of pollution to a 'virtuous cycle'?
- Do you know that five decades back pollution was not a big problem?
- It means our generation is responsible for the pollution problem. Do you agree, and why?
- A new global analysis released by the National Geographic Society finds that U.S. consumers rank last in a list of 17 nations on best sustainable behavior while India topped the list. Ironically, people in developing countries like India, China and Brazil were making the most sustainable choices, while consumers in the rich nations had the least sustainable lifestyles. What do you think is the problem with consumers in the U.S. and other rich nations?
- Why Lily didn't complete her part of the project? How Lily understood her responsibility towards her friends?
- Is it better to take responsibility and accept consequences or make an excuse to avoid consequences? Why?
- Accepting responsibility can improve your relationship with your friends. How?
- What does it mean to be a good friend?
- What does it mean when someone is described as a 'dependable' friend?
- Do you want to be considered as a 'dependable' friend? Why?
- What are the rewards for being a dependable friend?

We should be caring and loving to those whom we consider our good friends. Having good friends raises our self-confidence, empowering us to be the best we can be. It has been observed that usually popular children achieve better grades in schools. And in times of trouble, your friends can be the most important emergency service. You can depend on your true friends. That is why people with good friends are less likely to feel depressed.

Your identity is defined by your friends. Because we tend to pick up both good and bad characteristics from our friends, it is very important that we choose our friends wisely. We all know the old saying that you cannot choose your family, but you can choose your friends. So, choose wisely and choose carefully, because the people you decide to surround yourself with will have a great impact on your life. Remember, you can be friendly with all, but not all are acceptable as close friends. So, be selective and choose your friends intelligently as they will have a huge impact on the person you become.

Remember the time-tested adage, "Show me your friends and I'll tell you who you are."

10. The Bully and the Beast

Purpose of the Module: The idea is to help children understand that while confidence is a desirable trait, overconfidence is a dangerous thing. Overconfidence often backfires. Anyone can become a victim of overconfidence and narcissism. Students should appreciate the difference between confidence and overconfidence. And they should realize that the pursuit of knowledge is more important than the knowledge itself.

Key Values: Knowing Oneself, Humility.
Supplementary Values: Friendship, Modesty, Wisdom.
Life Skills: Common Sense, Quest for Knowledge.
Estimated Storytelling Time: 6 to 8 Minutes
Give-and-Take Session: 6 to 8 Minutes

Three school-time friends, Emmett, Edward and Jasper were doing a veterinary course at Cornell University. While Emmett and Edward were very studious and got good grades, Jasper was not so good in studies, but he was intelligent and wise. Jasper was a caring and sharing kind of person whereas Emmett was a big bully since middle school, and Edward was his crony who always followed his orders like a trained dog. Emmett and Edward were victims of pride and arrogance while Jasper was humble and full of common sense. He always behaved very sensibly.

Once during summer holidays, they decided to go on a trekking trip. They started early in the morning as they had planned to return by late evening.

When they reached midway, they decided to take lunch. As they were opening their Tiffin boxes under a shady tree, Jasper saw a giant bear lying nearby. At first glance, it looked dead. Emmett asked Edward to go and check. Once Edward reached there, he saw that the bear was badly hurt. Emmett and Jasper also came forward, and all the three friends began to inspect the injury.

After a while, Jasper said, "Let's get out of here before it regains consciousness."

Emmett teased, "Don't be such a coward. This is an excellent opportunity to test our veterinary skills. Edward, take out your water bottle and clean the wound so that I can inspect it."

Edward started working in a mechanical way, as he was told. Jasper again tried to reason with his friends, "Why are you getting involved in all this? We have not even completed our course, and we are not experienced. This is not a small mouse on which we can take risk. It is a big bear. We don't even have any instruments. Let's just get out of here."

Emmett retorted angrily, "I may have not completed my course but I already know what I need to know. I have learnt enough to treat this bear. I don't need any instruments. I know you are poor in studies. That's why you cannot understand what we are doing. I don't need any practice. I can prove my skills whenever I want. And if you are so scared feel free to leave anytime." Then Emmett started checking the wound again and Edward brought the first-aid box.

Jasper was upset and didn't know what to do. After a while he climbed a nearby tree and started tying two hiking ropes on its branches. He then called out to Edward and Emmett and said, "I have tied these two ropes for you both. If the bear wakes up and becomes violent, just climb up. You will be safe up here."

Emmett frowned, "Mr. Coward! Let us do our work."

After half an hour, they finished treating the bear. Then Emmett started poking the unconscious bear with a stick to see whether it wakes up or not. They wanted to check the result of their work. The bear suddenly woke up. When it saw two humans with sticks in their hands, it became violent. Edward and Emmett became terrified and started screaming for help. Jasper told them to climb up the tree. As they were climbing up, the bear first grabbed Edward and threw him back on the ground then he went towards Emmett and punched hard on his hips.

Seeing all this Jasper took out an apple from his bag and threw it on the bear's head. The bear's attention got diverted and he started growling at Jasper and then went after the apple.

In the meantime, Edward and Emmett climbed the tree. Once they were up, they started crying out of pain and cursing themselves for their foolishness. Jasper calmly said, "Don't fret. Now let's make a plan to get out of here safely."

They decided to wait for the bear to go far away before even thinking of climbing down. Emmett and Edward were in great pain. They couldn't even sit properly. They cured the bear but they were unable to cure their own wounds.

After an hour or so, the bear grew impatient. It looked angry and hungry. It again started growling. Edward and Emmett started trembling. Emmett, the big fat bully, even wet his pants because he was so scared. After almost half an hour of growling, the bear quietly went away in search of food. The three friends waited for some time and after making sure that there was no trace of the bear, they climbed down and quickly ran to the nearest road.

On the way, Emmett wondered aloud, "In life, knowledge is not everything. With knowledge, we must have the wisdom to use it well."

Give-and-Take Session

No one knows everything. And no one knows nothing. While you can't know everything there is to know, knowing what you know, and trying to know more is the right way to go forward. True knowledge is not how much knowledge you gain in the pursuit of knowing, but simply being in the pursuit of knowledge itself.

Intellectual humility is an intellectual virtue. It is an important aspect of intellectual growth. That is why since ancient times, the philosophers have recommended it

What Confucius said nearly 2500 years ago is just as true today: "To know that we know what we know, and that we do not know what we do not know, that is true knowledge." Socrates also made a similar argument that true knowledge is knowing that you do not know everything.

As the philosophers have taught us, it is important that we should know what we do not know. To be successful in life, we should have confidence but not overconfidence. Confidence is believing in yourself and your abilities. But overconfidence is believing in what you are not. Confidence is awareness of your knowledge as well as ignorance. Overconfidence is ignorance of your own ignorance. When confidence gives way to overconfidence, it transforms from an asset to a liability. So, confidence can help you realize your dreams but overconfidence can ruin your dreams.

In our search for confidence, it is not rare to reach a point where we become overconfident. There is a fine line between self-confidence and overconfidence. To put it simply, over-confidence is confidence that is unreasonable. The tale of Titanic is a classic example of how overconfidence backfires. Titanic's makers believed they had built an 'unsinkable' ship and, therefore, didn't require lifeboats for all the passengers.

The blockbuster movie 'Titanic' captured the imagination of the world with the touching themes of beauty, love and tragedy. The real story, which was overshadowed in the movie, is that it provides a morality tale. Many parts of the movie are not based on the recorded facts and are the result of 'artistic license' or 'commercial interests'. But then, a commercial movie is supposed to make money and not expected to clearly show the role of arrogance and overconfidence in the tragic tale.

The Titanic was supposed to be the largest and most luxurious ship ever built. Ironically, the 'unsinkable' was sunk on her maiden voyage. In the beginning, many passengers did not believe that the ship was sinking. They thought it was impossible, as claimed by the makers of the ship. In fact, the attitude of overconfidence that it was unsinkable led to the tragedy.

From ancient times to modern times, history is replete with examples of how overconfidence backfires. We all know that Hitler was a man of caliber with exceptional cleverness and managerial skills; but he lost due to his overconfidence. His arrogance and overconfidence brought him down in the end. The 2001 terrorist attack on the World Trade Center, the 2003 Iraq war, the 2008 financial crash and the killing of Osama are some recent examples of how overconfidence can backfire.

Points to Ponder
(It is not necessary for students to answer the questions or participate in discussion. They are just required to ponder over them. So, after every question or statement, a brief pause is recommended so as to allow their subconscious mind to absorb the desired values.)

- Jasper wanted to get away from the bear. Do you think he was a coward or animal hater? Why?
- Emmett provided first aid to the injured bear. Do you think he was a kind boy and animal lover?
- Emmett called Jasper coward. Who proved to be a real coward in the end?
- Jasper's nature and thinking was different from Emmett and Edward. How come he became their friend?
- When self-confidence, optimism and positive thinking are positive traits, why overconfidence is considered a negative trait?
- How we can strike the right balance between being confident and overconfident?
- Why Titanic episode is a good example showing the consequences of overconfidence? Think about some present day examples.
- We are drowning in information, but starved for knowledge. What are your views?

- Bertrand Russell said, "The whole problem with the world is that fools and fanatics are always so certain of themselves, but wiser people so full of doubts." Do you agree?
- One's tendency to be overconfident is shaped both by nature and nurture. What do you think?
- Overconfident people consider success as a destination and not as a journey. What are your views?

There is often a big difference between what people actually know and how much they think they know. Throughout the Bible we are told about the consequences of pride and arrogance. Proverbs 16:18 tells us that "pride goes before destruction, a haughty spirit before a fall." It means that someone who is full of pride is likely to fail in some way due to arrogance or overconfidence. And 1 Corinthians 10:12 says, "Wherefore let him that thinketh he standeth take heed lest he fall." It means that people who think they are standing firmly should be careful that they don't fall. It's important to note that all religions say the same things about pride, arrogance, ego, stubbornness and overconfidence.

Confidence is a good thing. It makes you strong. Children who have healthy self-confidence tend to enjoy life and make the most of opportunities. On the other hand, overconfident children often land up in unexpected trouble.

11. Beautiful Betty

Purpose of the Module: This section attempts to teach children about healthy body image. They should be encouraged to regard their bodies as an intelligent machine rather than merely as an object of beauty. Children should recognize that this machine requires fuel and maintenance to stay healthy and run properly, and healthy eating and regular physical activity play a vital role in maintaining this machine. And appearance is only one small part of what it takes to make a body better. Eating a balanced, nutritious diet is more important than overeating or restricting food. Children should be reminded that a positive, constructive approach will help them become healthy individuals.

Key Values: Healthy Living, Balance.
Supplementary Values: Healthy Eating, Simple Living, Self-esteem.
Life Skills: Healthy Body Image, Forward Looking, Good Manners.
Estimated Storytelling Time: 6 to 8 Minutes
Give-and-Take Session: 6 to 10 Minutes

Betty was a very beautiful girl. She was also very good in studies and extracurricular activities. Her friends considered her a perfect example of beauty with brains. Her schoolmates even nicknamed her 'Miss MBI International School' and 'Today's Cleopatra'. They praised her constantly, and she enjoyed all the attention.

Constant praise had quite turned the girl's head. She had become very conscious about her beauty. Gradually, she began to devote more time towards her looks. With little efforts from her side, the effect was great. People now started comparing her with top actresses.

She was very happy with the response she was getting. She started dreaming about her future. She decided she would become a supermodel and top actress. She started spending more time in front of mirror than with her books. As a result, her grades dropped from straight A's to B's and C's but she was too busy admiring her beauty to take care of that. She grew vain and careless.

Her parents began to worry about her because she was using so many synthetic beauty products at such a tender age. Earlier she believed in healthy and hygienic living. She also used to be an avid reader but now instead of buying books, she started spending all her monthly allowance on fashion accessories and other such stuffs. She started demanding more money for dresses, cosmetics, etc. since the hunger for such stuff is never ending.

But then, the ego has a way of never being satisfied. Its appetite grows with praise, compliments and flattery. And Betty was getting a continuous dose of flattery, which further fed her ego. As a result her vanity demanded more, and she made a list of all the things she wanted to change in her appearance. Her list had twelve points like making her nose a bit smaller, making her lips a bit fuller, lifting her eyebrows, reducing her waist by 3 inches and such other points.

One day as she was deciding what to wear for the school, God magically appeared in front of her. He told her that she had been a good girl and he was there to reward her. God said, "Ask for anything my dear child and I will grant it. But remember that once granted it can't be reversed. Think carefully because you can ask for any wish only today."

As soon as she overcame her initial shock, she ran to her drawer and took out the list of changes she wanted. Handing over the list to God, she politely requested, "These are my wishes. Please grant them."

God told her, "My child, think again. Is this the only thing you want in life? And remember it can't be reversed. So be sure of what you ask for."

Betty replied, "Father I have spent many days deciding it. This is all I want in life. I am sure of it as I think about it day and night. And these changes would make me look so beautiful why would I want to reverse them?"

God granted all her wishes and disappeared like a magic trick. She was very happy. She quickly ran to her mirror to check her new perfect look. But what she saw in the mirror shocked her. She could not recognize herself. Her eyes, her lips, everything was so different. She was no longer beautiful. She looked ugly. Her face looked like a plastic surgery gone horribly wrong. She cried very hard and desperately tried calling God. Suddenly, she realized what God told her earlier that day about irreversible wish. She started pounding on the floor and screaming.

Hearing her shouts, her mother came. She switched on the lights and saw that Betty was screaming and punching her bed. Her mother shook her. Betty woke with a start and started crying. She recounted her nightmare to her mother. Her mother hugged her and tried to calm her down.

"I promise Mom, I will change. I will become the old Betty again," she said trying to hide her embarrassment and added honestly, "I have realized I was on the wrong track, and I promise to correct myself from this very moment. I'm intelligent. I'm beautiful. Now my beauty regimen will be limited to avoiding junk food, eating a balanced diet of nutritious foods, and adopting a healthy lifestyle. I have a perfect life, and I promise to keep it that way."

Her mother was happy to see that her daughter had finally realized her mistake. Betty became her old self once again. Her grades improved. More importantly, she was happy and satisfied with her life.

Give-and-Take Session

Most of us have some issues with our bodies. We often have feelings of inadequacy and imperfection as we are bombarded by the media telling us we are too fat or too thin, or we aren't tall enough or too tall, etc. We all want to change a few things about our physical appearance. There is nothing wrong with it. After all, we are thinking animals for a reason. But it can become an issue if we start wasting our time and energy on such silly issues.

Many people feel unhappy with their body image, due to the image-destructive bombardment from the fashion industry. In a disturbing trend, various research findings show that body image problems are rapidly becoming more serious and widespread among children. The body image problems are resulting in eating disorders, mental illness, and low self-esteem, which are having disastrous consequences.

Many studies reveal that body image problems are more common in girls. Researchers at Glasgow University found that woman are up to 10 times more likely to feel unhappy with their body image than men. They often consider themselves as overweight even when they are at a healthy weight for their height. What's disturbing is that a study confirmed that children as young as 10 years old already have notions about the ideal body.

An obsession with body image can lead to serious illnesses. This mental disorder is more common in rich people, not sick people. Perhaps because they can afford to think about artificial means to improve their appearance. Or they think so. When we think about the victims of this disorder, the first name that comes to mind is Michael Jackson. He was a very gifted singer and entertainer. He enjoyed too much money and too much fame.

Jackson looked perfectly normal in his early years, before turning into the sideshow freak that he became later in his life. It is rumored that he may have had too many surgery procedures in his life. He had his nose done so many times that it caved in. Unhappy with his nose, he continued to indulge in nose jobs. It is also said that he got a chin implant, cheek implants, eyelid surgery, eyebrow lifting and skin lightening procedures. This drastically altered his appearance. There was nothing wrong with his former appearance as he had achieved fame as a singer since he was a child.

But like Betty, Jackson wanted to alter his appearance in many ways. Once Jackson said that he doesn't understand why everyone makes such a big deal about him getting plastic surgery, if everyone in Hollywood who has had plastic surgery went on vacation, it would be a ghost town. Deepak Chopra, a medical doctor and a close friend of Jackson, summed up Jackson's condition by saying: "What became his compulsion with cosmetic surgery was an expression of self-mutilation, a total lack of respect for himself."

We can't blame Jackson. Celebrities and models have their professional compulsions. It's their job to encourage us to buy whatever they're selling. In today's fiercely competitive world, they want to look perfect to do their job well. But we can't afford to blindly copy them. We need to maintain a sense of self respect.

Points to Ponder

- Why Betty's grades dropped from straight A's to B's and C's?
- Who was responsible for Betty's academic decline – Betty or her friends?
- The hunger for materialistic things is never ending, never satisfied. Do you agree?
- Just as the desire for materialistic things is created at an early age, so is the desire to learn. What do you think?
- How can flattery negatively affect us?
- Why Betty got such a dream?
- Betty was basically a good girl and her subconscious mind played a role in warning her through a dream. Do you agree?
- We should stay away from people who are keen to flatter us, as this is only feeding the ego. What do you think?
- We all have some issues with our appearance. But finding the confidence in yourself and getting healthy is all that matters. Do you agree? Why?
- How did Michael Jackson turn white? Why he took the risk of changing himself from a black to a white?
- Michael Jackson was a very successful singer and entertainer since childhood. Why he wanted to change his appearance?

Everyone wants to be attractive to others. Having a good personality is very important in today's high-pressure competitive world. Developing a good personality requires not only good looks but also a positive mental attitude. While we can only improve our looks to some extent, we have the ability to improve our personality as much as we want. Habits form personality, and personality shapes destiny. And the habits we acquire in our young age continue lifelong.

We need to follow a process to shift our negative energy to more positive thoughts, such as appreciating the parts of our bodies that we consider attractive. Even if we want to change a few things, it's important that we love our bodies. May God help us as we apply this process to developing good habits of the heart!

12. To Wear or Not To Wear

Purpose of the Module: This section is planned to emphasize that children ought to take a holistic, long-term view of their health issues. It's important for children to be health literate, and learning more is a great way for them to take responsibility for their health. They should appreciate that it's their basic responsibility to take good care of their body and adopt a healthy lifestyle so as to lead healthy, happy and productive lives.

Key Values: Responsibility to Self, Healthy Living.
Supplementary Values: Managing Peer Pressure, Sense of Right and Wrong.
Life Skills: Friendship, Self-awareness, Good Manners.
Estimated Storytelling Time: 5 to 7 Minutes
Give-and-Take Session: 6 to 10 Minutes

Lily's mother was very angry. She just got a call from Lily's best friend Betty. Betty told her that Lily was not wearing her glasses in school. Lily's mother used to think that her daughter was a responsible girl. She was shocked to know that Lily was not taking responsibility of her own health. She decided to talk to Lily in the evening.

As Lily came down for dinner, she observed that her daughter was looking troubled and upset. She asked her what the matter was. Lily told her that she had been getting headaches daily since past few days. Lily also told her mother that she was finding it difficult to study because of it.

Her mother turned towards her and enquired, "Betty has informed me that you are not wearing your glasses in the school. This Saturday you are coming with me to the eye doctor." Lily was shocked to hear that Betty had complained to her mom.

Her best friend betrayed her. She decided to confront Betty the next day. She hated going to the eye doctor as whenever she went there he told her that her power had increased. This had happened twice this year, and Lily didn't want it to happen again.

Next morning she talked to Betty. Actually, she just scolded Betty for complaining to her mother behind her back. She asked in disbelief, "What kind of a friend are you? How could you do this to me?"

Betty explained, "I'm your best friend, the kind of friend who cares. I did all this for your benefit."

Lily made a face and said, "Get lost and don't talk to me ever again." She was very angry and she stopped talking to Betty.

On Saturday, Lily reluctantly went to her eye doctor. After examining her, the doctor declared that her number had increased again, and it was not a good sign. Her father informed the doctor that she had been getting headaches in the school. The doctor asked Lily whether she was wearing her glasses or not. She nodded her head.

Then he turned towards her and asked, "Do you really wear them all the time?"

She told him that she wore them most of the time. The doctor pressed on, "Why not all the time?"

Poker-faced, Lily told him, "I look like an owl in glasses."

He asked, "What do you mean?"

She just shrugged her shoulders and said, "They just don't suit me."

He then asked whether someone in her school had teased her about it.

She blurted, "No, that's not the situation as I don't wear them in the school."

The doctor then explained her the importance of the specs. He gently said, "Lily you know that you have a responsibility to take care of your health and education. And this regular increase in your power is not a good sign at all. See your eyesight is yours and it is going to stay with you as long as you will live. You seem to be a responsible young lady. You should not compromise on such an important issue because of silly reasons. You must wear your glasses to improve your vision and life."

Lily thoughtfully said, "I will."

The doctor studied her response and said, "Good! And remember, not wearing specs can result in a difficult condition called lazy eye, wherein the stronger eye overtakes the other eye. And it becomes incurable with age."

Lily nodded. Then the doctor gave her a few real life examples where people suffered serious vision problems by ignoring specs at a young age.

Lily could relate to the examples of known persons. She understood the importance of glasses in her life. She started wearing them regularly. Initially, it was a bit awkward for her but slowly she got used to it. Many of her friends wore glasses. She thought that how stupid she was earlier, and how much time she had wasted to understand such a little issue.

As she wore her glasses regularly, her power stopped increasing. She realized that Betty was right and apologized to her. Betty forgave her and the two girls became best friends again.

Give-and-Take Session

Your body is the only vehicle you have been given for this ride called 'Life'. To ensure a longer, happier ride, you need to take good care of your body. In fact, it is your main responsibility to take good care of your body.

Remember, you have to live in your body for about 100 years. Yes, you heard it right. You are going to live that long, thanks to all the advances in the medical field. And proper health choices now will enable you to live a happier and healthier life as you age. So don't just think about today and tomorrow, but also about how today and tomorrow will affect your future.

The human body is a wonderful creation of God. And God has designed all body parts to work well till you live. But God's warranty is subject to two conditions. First, you will use your body parts responsibly. And the second, you will take good care of your health and all body parts.

Your body has many members: eyes, nose, heart, brain, tongue and ears to name just a few. And it is your prime responsibility to ensure that they are in perfect working condition.

Eyes are one of the most important organs in the human body and vision is one of the most wonderful gifts. With this amazing creation, you can see, feel and appreciate the beauty of this world. But often many of us ignore the importance of this vital organ and give little or no attention to eye care. When we are young and healthy, we tend to take our body for granted. We don't do anything to maintain it and sometimes even abuse it, until our body sends out signals that something is wrong.

Several studies confirm that about 20-25 % of children have undetected vision problems. Eighty percent of all learning is performed through vision. So it means over half a billion children suffer from undetected vision problems which are getting in the way of their learning.

Children with eye health problems face many barriers in life-academically, emotionally and socially. And it can affect everyday life experiences such as classroom learning, playing outdoor games, surfing the internet and playing video games. Children often do not know that they have a problem even if their vision is blurred or they have lazy eyes or some other eye problem. It is because they do not know what they 'should' be seeing.

Vision is the most critical of our five senses. And vision doesn't just happen. It is a learned process. A child's brain learns how to use eyes to see, just like it learns how to use hands to eat or legs to walk. Similarly, a child's brain learns to accommodate the vision problem. That's why it is very important for children to get their eyes examined on a regular basis. They should also get their eyes checked if they notice any of these signs:

? Frequent headaches
? Eye strain, burning, itching, or watery eyes
? Loss of concentration
? Sensitivity to light or glare
? Difficulty in adjusting to dark rooms
? Difficulty in focusing on objects
? Dry eyes with itching or burning sensation
? Dislike for reading or writing
? Holding book too far or too close from face
? Making frequent change in distance at which book is held
? Hard to copy from the board
? Leaving out small words when reading
? Losing place while reading
? Hard to pay attention when reading
? Confusing words or letters

Regular eye examinations can catch many of these problems and help you keep your vision healthy. When left untreated, these vision conditions can interfere with your learning. What's more, vision problems often negatively influence self-esteem, which further impairs academic performance.

Points to Ponder

- Why Lily didn't wear her specs in the school?
- Why Lily had been getting headaches daily?
- Betty complained to Lily's mom about Lily's irresponsible behavior. Do you think Betty betrayed her best friend?

- You should behave responsibly when it comes to what you put into your body and what you do with it. Do you agree? Why?
- Do you think of your body as a machine that requires the same attention to regular checks and maintenance that you give to your car? Why?
- Do you realize that looking after your health can empower you to have greater control over your quality of life?

History shows that children who get teased in school grow up to become more successful in life than the children who tease them. Weak children engage in teasing behavior because they often consider it a tool to hide their insecurities. When it comes to health and body image, smart children don't care about such morally weak people. Such confident children have good self-esteem. They don't give away their personal power to others. It doesn't matter to them what others say. They know that they have a responsibility to take good care of their body.

Love your body, take care of it and it will be sure to return the favors.

13. Future We Don't Want

Purpose of the Module: This section aims to make students aware of the deteriorating condition of our environment, and what they can do to help improve it. It also seeks to sensitize them about the urgent need for conservation of environment and its resources to maintain harmony in the environment. The objective is to remind them about what a difference a healthy environment can make in our life, and to create a generation of students who are passionate about the environment.

Key Values: Respect for the Environment, Social Responsibility.
Supplementary Values: Forward Looking, Common Cause, Simple Living.
Life Skills: Cooperation, General Knowledge, Planning for the Future, Sharing.
Estimated Storytelling Time: 6 to 8 Minutes
Give-and-Take Session: 7 to 11 Minutes

Peter was on cloud nine. He just came to school in his car. The car looked brand new with a new paint job and spruced up interiors, but James noticed that smoke was coming out of the exhaust pipe. James asked Peter, "What's wrong with your car?"

For a moment Peter was taken aback. He said, "What do you mean? It is all right. There is not a scratch or dent anywhere. I just got it painted."

James said, "But why is the smoke coming out from the exhaust pipe? Did you get your engine and everything checked?"

Peter told James the story of his car. He said, "No. I didn't. Actually, it is my dad's old car. He was selling it but I asked him to give it to me. He told me it's not in the right condition but I really wanted a car. He gave me money to get it fixed. I got a paint job done and got a new stereo. The old one had a bad reception. I didn't bother about the engine. I mean its running all right so why should I waste money on it."

James told Peter that it's wrong, and he should get it fixed. James tried to reason with him, but Peter argued that why should he get it fixed when it's running all right. James told him that he should see how it's harming the environment, and how it's harming our future.

James further remarked, "The gas coming out of your car is probably carbon dioxide or worst carbon monoxide, which is a poisonous gas. Since carbon dioxide is a greenhouse gas, increasing the amount of carbon dioxide in the atmosphere will increase the temperatures of our earth. Carbon dioxide emissions, methane and deforestation are slowly raising the temperature of our earth. Global warming induced climate change is one of our biggest challenges," James paused to see the reaction on Peter's face.

After confirming the effect of his words, he continued his passionate preaching, "In fact, most human activities generate carbon dioxide. Even breathing generates carbon dioxide. While we can't stop or reduce breathing, there are other ways we can adopt to reduce our carbon footprint. Remember, prevention is better than cure. And if we don't behave in a more responsible way, there may not be any cure for our grandchildren. The future we want for our future generations depends on us. We must remember that we do not inherit the earth from our ancestors, but borrow it from our children."

Peter finally realized his folly and said, "Ok, I see you have a point. I have read it many times that air pollution is one of the most serious problems, and vehicular pollution is considered to be a major source of air pollution. And now the earth's atmosphere has more than 400 parts per million of carbon dioxide which varied between 180 and 300 parts per million in the pre-industrial period. I shudder to think of the consequences. Now I realize that I must get the engine fixed but the point is I have already spent all the money dad gave me in improving the look of the car. I don't have any money left now. I can't afford to get it fixed."

James quipped, "Now I hope you understood the meaning of Voldemort's comment to Snape in yesterday's movie 'I don't know why you want me to destroy the earth. Muggles are doing a great job on their own'. Just think of it even Dumbledore preferred to die as he was aware that even his magic and wisdom could not convince Muggles to mend their wayward ways."

Then James told him on a serious note that he could get a part-time job for a few weeks at a nearby mall or food joint. It would help him save the required money as well as give him some work experience. James further added, "Even I will work with you. That way I will also be able to do my bit for the environment. After all, we are going to enjoy this car together. If we work together, we will save twice the money. And working would be fun when we will do it together."

Both friends worked hard for six weeks and saved enough money to get the engine fixed. When they got the car engine fixed, they were really happy. Can you guess why?

It was a sense of satisfaction. They were proud to do their share for cleaner air.

Give-and-Take Session

We human beings tend to forget how far we have come in a comparatively very short period of time. Though we have been around for more than 300000 years, most of the development took place in the 20th century, including environmental degradation. The amazing advances in science and technology during the past few decades have changed the way we live and work. But, despite these advances, we face a major crisis on our planet earth, our only home. And we're not sure if we should celebrate or feel sorry for our future generations. Environmental degradation has assumed alarming proportions. And pollution has become a major threat to the very existence of mankind on earth.

The mother earth was once a fabulous place to live. Our

irresponsible behavior has polluted it to such an extent that the pollution has not only become the root cause of many diseases, but it is increasingly making normal living difficult. Here are some pointers to understand the problem.

> Worldwide, 2000–2009 was the warmest decade ever recorded.
> If the earth keeps getting warmer, up to one-fourth of the entire world's plants and animals could become extinct within 100 years.
> Transportation and electricity generation cause more than 60 percent of the greenhouse gas emissions.
> Our earth is getting warmer because people are adding heat-trapping gases to the atmosphere, mainly by burning fossil fuels.
> According to the conservative estimates of renowned biologist E.O. Wilson, we cause the extinction of an average of 100 species per day.
> The U.S. State Department estimates that forests, four times the size of Switzerland are lost each year because of clearing and degradation.
> The World Bank reports that 80 countries are experiencing water shortages serious enough to threaten agriculture, and their water shortages may soon become food shortages.
> In the past 30 years, we have consumed 30% of the earth's natural resources.
> According to the World Resources Institute, more than 80 percent of the earth's natural forests have already been destroyed.
> The WHO estimates that 24% of global disease burden and 23% of all deaths can be attributed to environmental factors.

Here too we are very efficient. All this we have achieved in the past few decades. Really, we have come a long way relatively in a very short period of time. The earth is about 4.5 billion years old. Humans have been on the earth for only about 300,000 years. And the earth has been just right for life till a few decades back. We polluted the 4.5 billion-years-old earth in just 50 years. Looks like an incredible achievement! Don't you think so?

We face a dangerous threat from the changes our own pollution has caused on the earth's climate. We know what is to be done and agree that something needs to be done urgently about global warming and climate change. And most of us also agree that the threats we face are real, immediate and immense. We all like to think we are green. But when it comes to protecting our environment, the first stumbling block, however, is that nobody is ready to really sacrifice. All want to continue their indulgences.

Protecting our environment is our responsibility since we live in it and use its resources. Protecting our environment is the same as protecting our house. Remember, we can afford a new house, but we can't have a new environment.

Points to Ponder

- Why Peter spent money on the look of his car and not on the engine of his car?
- Do you know your parents and teachers' generation is responsible for most of the environmental degradation? How do you propose to make amends for their unintentional, irresponsible behavior?
- Everyone is affected by the quality of our air. Which people in particular are likely to become sick from air pollution?
- What is the Greenhouse Effect?
- We know that saving energy and recycling whatever we can are significant ways of protecting the environment. Can you identify the best ways to save energy and recycle products in your home?
- Why the environment is deteriorating in spite of all-round efforts to protect it?
- Half of the reason why the environment is deteriorating is because we are constantly burning up fossil fuels to produce new things. Do you agree?
- Why environment protection hype and pollution have been increasing in tandem, more or less in the same proportion?
- Is the government doing enough to protect the environment?

- In our society, carbon footprints of a person determine his or her status. Do you think such high-status people need medical attention, or they should be considered as criminals?

We must keep in mind that all our efforts in the education and other areas will be useless, if there is no future for the earth itself. We must take a holistic view of the grim situation owing to the imminent danger of the global warming and its serious consequences. We must remember that the earth was not given to us by our parents; it is loaned to us by our children.

Before our so-called development, nature's own systems kept the air and water fairly clean. With increasing urbanization and industrialization, we started to release more pollutants into the atmosphere than nature could handle. Now nature cannot cope with the pollution without our help. Our environment is precious and important. It can't speak for itself so it is up to us to protect it.

As caring children of the mother earth, each one of us needs to persuade ourselves to at least contribute our share. We must do our part to make sure that the air we breathe, the earth we grow things in and the water we drink do not become polluted.

14. Runaways Never Win, Winners Never Run Away

Purpose of the Module: This story is planned to sensitize students about the evils of drinking and the importance of abstinence. Students should realize that they are living in an exciting age, where protective walls of family values are not strong enough to withstand the pressures of peers and media, which often influence their decisions and lifestyles. Present times call for greater responsibility and strength of character on their part.

Key Values: Abstinence, Perseverance.
Supplementary Values: Self-reliance, Faithfulness, Forgiveness.
Life Skills: Courage, Devotion, Forward Looking.
Estimated Storytelling Time: 6 to 8 Minutes
Give-and-Take Session: 7 to 12 Minutes

Emily was abandoned by her husband. She had a one-year old son. Her alcoholic husband left her for another woman because she strongly opposed his heavy drinking. He took all the cash and cashable items with him to start his new life. Poor Emily was emotionally shattered. She was also scared about her and her son's future. She had no work experience and no other means of supporting herself and her son. She often thought about suicide, but she believed that it was an option for cowards, and she was not a coward. She decided to find meaning in life, and resolved to hang on for the sake of her son.

One of her childhood friends was an elementary school teacher. She approached her for help. Her teacher friend gave her some money to sustain and got her enrolled in a vocational course.

After six months, the course was complete. Emily with the help of her friend opened a small restaurant, which served popular fast food items like burgers and hotdogs. Initially, she did all the work from cooking to selling herself to save some money. Gradually her restaurant gained popularity as she served nutritious and hygienic food at a reasonable price.

After a year, she employed two persons, one as a cashier and one as a cook. Time passed by and she hired some more people to meet the demand.

When her son Tom turned four, she got him enrolled in a good school. On his first day, Tom was very excited, and she personally dropped him off at the school. Other kids came with both their father and mother, and her son got a bit upset seeing that. That day when Tom returned from school, he asked her about where his father was. Emily could not tell him the truth at such a tender age. She just told him that he's no more with us. He inquired, "Where is he?"

She merely replied, "He's gone forever and now you shouldn't waste your time thinking about him. Go and play."

After some time, her restaurant was doing good business. So, she decided to expand her business. From the profits she had made in the last few years, she opened two more restaurants. Because of her goodwill, new restaurants were instant success.

As Tom grew, he would often ask her about his father but she avoided the topic. Sometimes, he taunted her saying that she had thrown him out. She thought that it would be better not to tell him the real story at this age.

Considering his mother's tough life as a single parent and entrepreneur, Tom wanted her to marry again. To start the topic, once he asked her, "What do you think of the word marriage."

"Marriage is not a word; it is a sentence," his mother quipped and jumped into another subject.

Her business was going great. She hired many people to look after her big chain of restaurants. Her teacher friend, who got her enrolled in the vocational course, was very happy to see her success. Once she met Emily's son at their restaurant. Tom was drinking beer and looked sad. He recognized her and greeted her. She asked him what the matter was. He told her that his friends were teasing him about his father. Tom said, "I just want to know the truth but mother always avoid telling me about that."

She told him to come with her. As they were going in her car, she said, "I am going to show you your father but before that you must know the truth. You are a big boy now, and you have the right to know the truth."

She told him how his alcoholic father had left his mother for another woman and how his mother had single-handedly built such a big business chain while taking good care of him. She also told him that his father was an engineer and not a bad guy till he started drinking.

She stopped the car and told him that they have reached their destination. Tom got out and was surprised to see that they have come to another of his mother's restaurant. She took him inside and they sat on a corner table. From there she pointed to the guard, who had just welcomed them, and said, "You see that guard at the entrance? He is your father."

Tom was shocked to hear the truth. But he didn't feel like meeting the man who preferred alcohol over his wife. In fact, he was ashamed of him since he left his mother for another woman. Trying to hide his anger, he asked her, "Did mother give him the job?"

She replied, "No she didn't. The manager of this restaurant employed him, but your mother knows that he works here and she has no objection."

When Tom went home, he asked his mother, "Why did you give job to that scoundrel?"

His mother told him, "I have nothing to do with him as he has broken something special and betrayed us. Perhaps alcohol was responsible for his deeds. Drinking alcohol spoils not only one's health but also the whole family. It robs us of our ability to think rationally. However, he has a family with kids. And forgiveness helps us move on in life."

Hearing this, Tom replied, "Mom you are great, and I would like to be like you one day. And I promise I will never touch alcohol in my life."

Give-and-Take Session

The British soul singer, Amy Winehouse died from alcohol poisoning at the age of 27. An inquiry into her death found that she had more than five times the legal driving limit of alcohol in her body.

Singer Whitney Houston died from taking a lethal cocktail of prescription drugs and alcohol. When she tragically died at the Beverly Hilton Hotel, a deadly mixture of drugs and alcohol was found in her system.

Jackson Pollock was an alcoholic who died in a drunk driving accident at a young age. He was a great painter and one of the most influential twentieth century artists. His painting No. 5, 1948 was sold as the most expensive painting ever for about 140 million dollars.

Rodney King was found dead at the bottom of his pool, after a lifelong battle with drug and alcohol addiction.

Alexander the Great, as famed for his drinking as for his military exploits was the first publicly acknowledged alcoholics in the human history. Many believe that his drinking bouts led to his death at the age of 32.

These are just a few examples of successful people who lost everything because of one bad habit, or we can say a disease. They all were talented people who knew that drinking alcohol was not good for their health and career. And this list can go on and on, but I hope you got the point.

Drinking alcohol is dangerous, especially for youngsters. Alcohol is a drug, and it is the drug most abused by youngsters. Alcohol kills more teenagers than all other drugs combined. People drink because they enjoy the way it makes them feel. They use alcohol to boost their self-confidence, to relieve stress, or to forget their problems. They don't realize that these are short term feelings. The alcohol users try to forget about their worries for a while, but this is a temporary solution, which often creates more problems in their life.

When people drink too much or too often, they become dependent on alcohol. This is called alcohol addiction, or alcoholism. Remember, addiction is craving fulfillment from something that cannot provide fulfillment. Alcoholism is a serious disease just as drug addiction is. While some think that being addicted to alcohol is not as serious as being addicted to heroin, it can still affect your health in ways you never even thought of. Alcoholism is a progressive disease which affects the lives of millions of people including friends and family members of alcoholics. Most alcoholics are in denial about their condition, and often hide their behaviors from their loved ones. Irresponsible use of alcohol can lead to many adverse consequences in a person's life. Some examples are:
- ➤ Impaired brain development
- ➤ Decline in academic performance
- ➤ Injury or death
- ➤ Fighting or brawling
- ➤ Violent or abusive behavior
- ➤ Drowning
- ➤ Drug overdose
- ➤ Binge drinking
- ➤ Arrest for driving under the influence of alcohol
- ➤ Self-harm or suicide

There is no cure for alcoholism, but there is a treatment. Since it is a progressive disease, it always gets worse without treatment.

Alcohol is a neurotoxin, which means it can poison the brain. One of the effects of excessive alcohol use is that it interferes with vitamin B absorption, which in turn prevents the brain from working properly.

Points to Ponder

- Why Emily's husband left her?
- Why Emily never entertained the thought of suicide?
- Why Emily's ex-husband, a trained engineer was working as a guard?
- We live in a world where forgiveness and moving on is seen as weakness and fighting for justice is seen as strength. What do you think?
- Alcoholism is an equal opportunity destroyer. Do you agree? Why?
- Alcohol addiction is a bad habit or a disease? Why?

Many surveys found peer pressure is directly responsible for an increase in risky behaviors among children, including cigarette smoking, drug abuse and drinking alcohol. Peer Pressure is a major contributor to the initiation and continuation of alcohol or other drug use.

Peer pressure affects everyone at one time or another. Children give in to pressure from peers and first take alcohol to gain acceptance of children who already drink. Here are some reasons why or how that happens.
- Want to be liked by others
- Want to appear grown up
- Don't want to be made fun of
- Don't want to lose a friend
- Don't want to hurt someone's feelings
- Aren't sure of what you really want
- Fear of being rejected by others
- Don't know how to get out of the situation

Making smart choices include being able to stand up to peer pressure. You can use these tips to prepare yourself to face peer pressure and win the game.

- ➤ Know your limits, and let other people know those limits too. Know where you stand on important issues like alcohol and drugs, and do not allow anyone to make you change your position.
- ➤ Keep in mind that you don't have to do anything you don't want to do.
- ➤ Gain the mental edge by preparing yourself ahead of time for sticky situations.
- ➤ Never be afraid to speak up and politely assert your boundaries.
- ➤ Remember, giving in to peer pressure isn't going to help you.
- ➤ Seek out friends with interests, beliefs, and values similar to your own.
- ➤ When faced with a tough decision, consider the long-term consequences of your actions. If required, don't hesitate to seek help from an adult you trust.

It is important that you do what you feel is right for you. But decide wisely. All the best!

15. The Wrong Turn

Purpose of the Module: This story is planned to emphasize that our decisions affect our life and they should not be influenced by peer pressure. The aim is to encourage students to avoid the pitfalls of negative peer pressure, and make them aware that while making choices gives us freedom, it is also a big responsibility.

Key Values: Responsibility to Self, Sense of Right and Wrong, Managing Peer Pressure.
Supplementary Values: Self-reliance, Initiative.
Life Skills: Decision Making, Career Planning.
Estimated Storytelling Time: 5 to 7 Minutes
Give-and-Take Session: 6 to 12 Minutes

Lucy was an intelligent girl who got good grades. When the time for choosing her career stream came, she got confused. She had not applied her mind to this issue. Her mother suggested one career field, and her father suggested another. Different teachers recommended different career lines. She became more and more confused.

So she decided to consult her friends. They had done a lot of research on various career options. They had also consulted many seniors and professionals. She was glad to have such friends. Her three best friends were taking the engineering stream. They talked continuously about its prospects, and what a great future they would have after doing it. She also liked science. Finally, she decided to follow her friends, as they seemed to be much more knowledgeable about the career planning process. What's more, she would get to enjoy their company. In fact, she was a victim of peer pressure since primary school.

Initially everything was good. They enjoyed learning science. But after a few weeks, Lucy found it difficult to cope up with the heavy workload. Compared to her friends, she would take more time to pick up physics and math. There was so much to learn and so little time. She took science because of her friends, but they rarely had time for fun. Lucy's grades began to drop. She tried hard. But, somehow the more she tried, the more her grades went down.

Her parents got worried. They arranged a private tutor for physics and math. But the move backfired. Tuitions further put pressure on her time and mind. She got so terrified of her bad grades that at the time of giving her tests, she would become anxious and nervous. While giving tests, her heartbeat would accelerate, and she would have hard time breathing. Sometimes her mind would become blank, and she would literally feel like a vegetable.

Her best friend Miley knew that Lucy was not cut out for science. She also knew Lucy had very good command over language and literature, and enjoyed writing fiction since she was a child. So, she suggested to Lucy to consult the school counselor about her grades.

Lucy took an appointment with the school counselor. She discussed the problem with him and requested a solution.

The counselor asked, "Did you really choose science stream from your mind and heart?"

Lucy then recounted the whole story of her stream selection process.

The counselor analyzed the Lucy's case and said, "Lucy selecting the right stream is not a difficult process. You should make a list of your interests and talents and accordingly take a stream. I advise you to select a stream suitable for you, and not based on what your friends have taken. Many students opt for wrong careers due to peer pressure. It is still not very late. Career should be decided on the basis of what you could do well rather than what you would like to do. It should be decided on the basis of your skills, talents and aptitude. There is no point in choosing a lucrative and highly paying field and performing badly in it. You should change your stream based on your talents and abilities. After you take a smart decision, request the principal. And this time don't consult your friends. Consult your mind and heart to take a rational decision. You are an intelligent girl. I am sure you would take the right decision."

After careful consideration of her strengths and wisely exploring various career options, Lucy decided to opt for journalism. She had a good command over the English language and a creative bent of mind. She was sad about wasting one year. She resolved to work hard to make up for the time lost and quickly climb the career ladder.

Lucy later became a senior journalist with a leading newspaper. She followed her heart and success followed her. Moreover, she was happy and satisfied in her career.

Give-and-Take Session

Lucy made a wrong career choice because her friends were taking science. Taking wrong decisions because of peer pressure is very common. Sometimes children choose the wrong career under the influence of friends and regret later. Some realize in time and change the direction to limit their losses.

Like Lucy, one of the most popular stars in the world, Tom Cruise also changed his career after one year. Tom Cruise wanted to become a Catholic priest and even attended a Franciscan seminary when he was 14, but abandoned those plans after one year. Many people make wrong choices. What's important is realizing your mistake as early as possible.

At age 30, Harrison Ford was a carpenter before he hit the big screen. And at age 30, Jesus also finally stopped doing carpentry and began preaching and performing miracles. See, Harrison Ford and Jesus have more in common than you'd think.

Every person is unique. Everyone has their own abilities and limitations. You should not blindly follow others. You should know your strengths and weaknesses, and make your goals accordingly. By blindly following your friends, neither you will get success nor happiness. Don't give into peer pressure. Take your own decisions. Follow your heart. That way you won't regret your choices later in life.

Swami Vivekananda explained it beautifully by saying: "We are responsible for what we are, and whatever we wish ourselves to be, we have the power to make ourselves. If what we are now has been the result of our own past actions, it certainly follows that whatever we wish to be in the future can be produced by our present actions; so we have to know how to act."

Points to Ponder
(It is not necessary for students to answer the questions or participate in discussion. They are just required to ponder over them. So, after every question or statement, a brief pause is recommended so as to allow their subconscious mind to absorb the desired values.)

- While selecting her subjects, Lucy was seeking advice from her friends, parents and teachers. Why she was not asking herself this question? Why she was not considering her talents and abilities?
- Why private tuitions could not help Lucy to improve her performance?
- When Lucy realized her mistake, she changed her subjects and wasted one year. Was it a correct decision?
- Would you like Tom Cruise as an actor or as a priest?
- How can we withstand the pressures of peers and society and make responsible choices?
- How peer pressure can play a positive role in your life?
- How peer pressure can play a negative role in your life?

It's normal for children to adopt all that is considered hip and cool without a second thought. They don't do it deliberately. They just can't make out the difference between the good and the bad. But to succeed in life, they need to understand the difference. They need to know how to handle the negative peer pressure.

Young teens and preteens are in a particularly vulnerable situation. They are enjoying new freedoms and experiencing new feelings. But they don't have the experience to handle many situations they confront. They don't know how to handle the peer pressure or resist other temptations of life.

Staying away from the peers is not a solution. And banning or isolating peers is also not the solution. Best solution is learning to make good choices in life. But then, there are many intelligent students who benefit from peer pressure

Peer pressure is not always bad. It can actually teach you the right way of living. It can guide you to change yourself for the better. Looking at what others do, can help you bring about a positive change in your way of thinking. If you are intelligent enough to pick selectively, peer pressure can actually result in a positive change in your life.

While positive peer pressure leads to progress and healthy competition amongst teenagers, negative peer pressure can cause a host of problems that may range from lack of focus in academics to falling in the trap of unhealthy habits. Negative peer pressure may prompt you to take wrong decisions. With good friends, you are likely to adopt good habits and give up bad habits.

16. Every Day is Mother's Day

Purpose of the module: This story is designed to create an appreciation of caring atmosphere of family and remind children about their responsibility to their family. It seeks to reinforce from early ages the basics of responsibility and time management. Children who care for their family members develop a sense of belonging and their confidence grows as their abilities grow. And caring for family members creates a sense of oneness.

Key Values: Responsibility to Family, Self-reliance, Caring.
Supplementary Values: Cooperation, Initiative, Balance, Responsibility to Self.
Life Skills: Time Management, Planning and Organizing, Discipline.
Estimated Storytelling Time: 6 to 8 Minutes
Give-and-Take Session: 6 to 12 Minutes

Matthew and his twin sister Christy were very disturbed. Whenever they asked their mother to play with them, she was busy doing something. She always told them that many chores were pending, and she would play after completing them. But she never got any time before 10 PM. And it was her rule that the children should sleep by 10 PM. They got bored playing with each other. There was no challenge as they were more or less on the same level. They were equally good or equally bad at different games. So it was not much fun as there was not any real competition.

They had repeatedly tried to convince their mother to play with them. No matter how much they bribed, begged, flattered and threatened her, she always refused. She would not budge. Her silly chores were more important to her.

On the mother's day, the class teacher gave them a project. The topic was time management. They had to make their 24-hour schedule. Then they were supposed to find ways to manage their time better so as to get some spare time for fun and creative activities. Lastly, they had to write how they planned to use that extra time.

It was an interesting project. Everyone got busy in making his or her timetable. Many students realized how much time they actually spend watching TV or surfing the internet, while some realized how little time they spend studying. Matthew and Christy had an almost perfect timetable with good balance between studies and entertainment. They had around one hour left in their day, which Matthew planned to allot to any creative activity and Christy decided to devote her spare time to any social work. They finished their project first. The teacher was impressed with their timetables.

The class was still doing the project so both of them decided to make timetables for their parents. Christy said, "Dad already has a fixed daily schedule. Let's make one for mom and see why she never has any time left?"

Matthew replied, "Good idea."

Both of them made a rough timetable of their mother's activities. They were surprised to find that half the time she was busy doing things that they were supposed to do like cleaning their room, arranging their cupboard, etc. They were shocked to see on paper how much work their mother alone had to do.

Matthew said, "It is really mean of us to play and enjoy while mom do our work."

Christy replied in a dull tone, "Yes, you are right. Hey, why don't we help mother in that one-hour time we have at our leisure? That way we will be using it well and mom will also get some time to relax."

Matthew got excited and said, "That sounds great and if we both work one hour then mom will save two hours. One hour we will tell her to take rest or enjoy activities that she likes and the other one hour she can play with us."

Finally, they found a way to get their mother listen to them. If her chores were finished in time, she would not take any excuse. She had to play with them. And they all would have more fun things to do.

They went home and cleaned their room. Then they arranged their cupboard, books, gadgets, etc. That evening when their mother came to clean the room, she was surprised to see it spic and span. The children came running to her and hugged her.

Matthew said, "We realized why you never had any time to play with us. We will try to do our own work."

Their mother was very happy. She smiled through her tears as she saw the poster on the wall 'Every Day is Mother's Day.' The three of them went to the living room and played monopoly. Their mother won but the children finally got someone to compete with and improve their game. All three of them were laughing and enjoying. When their dad came, he was pleasantly surprised to see such a scene. He also sat down to play with them.

From then onwards, the family regularly played together and spent quality time with each other.

Give-and-Take Session

Children all over the world wonder how they can make their parents happy. One simple way is to take good care of your tasks and help your parents with household chores. It's a good way of showing that you love and care for them. Remember, doing chores instills a sense of responsibility that will also help you in other areas of your life.

When you look around, you will find most successful people understood their responsibility to the family early in life. And there are many true stories of celebrities where they made a name for themselves in the process of helping their parents.

Versace is one of the top fashion brands, and its founder Gianni Versace was one of the best-known fashion designers of the twentieth century. His mother was the family's main provider, tailoring clothes to make a living. Versace used to help his mother as she embroidered dresses, finding gold braids and precious stones for her. He gradually began designing garments himself and eventually excelled at playing fashion designer to Hollywood. Princess Diana, Elton John and Madonna were just a few of his illustrious clients.

Eoin (*pronounced Owen*) Colfer is the famous author of the hugely successful Artemis Fowl books. His novels are often compared to the works of J. K. Rowling and are described as James Bond with fairies. His mother was a drama teacher and a local actor. He used to help his mother learn her lines and other things. Eoin believes that this practice has helped him develop his quick, dry wit, which has put his books at the top of many bestseller lists, making this Irish primary school teacher a millionaire international celebrity.

If you look around, you will find many such examples. Be it Bill Gates, Steve Jobs, Warren Buffet, Richard Branson, Steven Spielberg, or any other success story, they all improved their key skills at a very young age.

Points to Ponder

- Matthew's mother gave more importance to household chores than to playing with her children. Was it right on her part?
- Why time management is an important skill for everyone?
- Why it is important to have a right balance between studies and entertainment in your schedule?
- To spend your time wisely is to spend your life wisely, to waste your time is to waste your life. Do you agree?
- Learning a skill in early years like Versace and Eoin has many benefits. Do you agree?
- Why most successful people – tech icons like Bill Gates, empire builders like Richard Branson and legendary investment gurus

like Warren Buffett – start their career at a very young age? Why do they become generous donors when they reach the top?

- Eoin was a primary school teacher. Do you think his association with kids helped him in his writing career? If yes, how?

When you understand the importance of your responsibility to your family, you start responding and helping, rather than reacting and criticizing. Acceptance of family responsibility is the point from where you can begin improving your lot and that of other family members. It will give you satisfaction and happiness. Try it out.

There is no doubt that time spent worrying or complaining is the biggest time waster. Avoid negative thoughts. Think about how you can make things better for yourself. Complaining behavior restricts you; taking responsibility helps you get what you want in life. Try to spend quality time with family members. Quality time means any activity that shows your parents you like them, care about them, and love them.

To succeed, it is necessary to use your time properly. Remember everyone has 24 hours in a day. When you organize your time and schedule, you will notice that your environment has been completely transformed. It becomes a positive, nourishing environment, which helps you to do your tasks more efficiently.

We conclude today's discussion with the words of Marge Kennedy, "In truth a family is what you make it. It is made strong, not by number of heads counted at the dinner table, but by the rituals you help family members create, by the memories you share, by the commitment of time, caring, and love you show to one another, and by the hopes for the future you have as individuals and as a unit."

17. Was iPhone Worth It?

Purpose of the Module: Students ought to appreciate that the major differentiation between animals and humans is our ability to make rational decisions, and that would often mean overcoming our desires. Desires are part of human nature, but human desires often go beyond the reasonable level. A person who is more in control over his desires and emotions would be able to succeed in life easily.

Key Values: Sense of Right and Wrong, Managing Peer Pressure.
Supplementary Values: Self-restraint, Simple Living.
Life Skills: Common Sense, Discipline.
Estimated Storytelling Time: 5 to 7 Minutes (The story is inspired from some real life incidents)
Give-and-Take Session: 5 to 8 Minutes

A young boy named Liam wanted an iPhone. Some of his schoolmates had it. He was jealous of them and the attention they received from other fellow students. He craved the attention they got. He belonged to a lower middle-class family. He asked his father to give him money so that he could buy an iPhone. But his father refused because his budget was tight. However, his father patted him and said, "Son you are in the second half of your last school year. Only four months are left before your finals. You should focus on your studies right now and not on such things. A new gadget will only divert your attention. You study well and get admission in a good college, and I will try my best to arrange money for it."

Liam was disappointed, as he didn't want to wait for another four months. Moreover, then he would not get a chance to show it off to his school buddies. He decided to do something about the money himself. He shared his thoughts with Sam, his best friend. Sam suggested that he could work in a nearby restaurant or mall to save money. But Liam didn't like this idea as this could take months. He wanted to get an iPhone soon. He didn't have the patience to wait for it. His immature mind was ready to do anything to get it.

Liam recalled that his uncle had once donated one of his kidneys to his grandfather. At that time, the doctors had informed them that humans could survive on one kidney. His uncle donated his kidney four years ago. His uncle was hale and hearty. He decided to sell his kidney.

But then, after exploring he realized it was not possible. No good doctor of any reputed hospital would do such a surgery. As he was not donating but selling the kidney, it would be considered illegal.

But Liam was adamant. He decided to explore some other way to sell his kidney. He looked for any greedy doctor who could buy his kidney. Within a week, he could find some people who posed as doctors in a nearby village. They were not bona-fide doctors, but they treated innocent villagers and poor people.

Liam contacted one of them and told him that he wanted to sell his kidney. The so-called doctor told him that he had to involve some other persons who would arrange someone who needed a kidney transplant. Liam told him that he wanted a good deal. The phony doctor assured him that they would get him the best deal.

The doctor contacted Liam after a week and asked him to meet them. Liam went to their clinic, and they told him that they could find a great deal for him. He was told that he would be getting $2000. Liam thought that the money was less and asked them how much they were keeping. They told him that they were just keeping $500 for operation and other expenses.

Liam asked them to extract more money from the buyer. But they told him that the man who had agreed to buy the kidney was poor and could not afford more. And it was the only available deal. Liam thought that the money was less but still sufficient for his iPhone. He agreed and donated his kidney. He decided to buy his new iPhone next week. Perhaps he would buy an iPad as well.

Next day, Liam started feeling uncomfortable. He thought it was just some temporary side-effects. But instead of getting better, his condition started to deteriorate. He had no option but to inform his parents. He told his father that he had sold his kidney to buy an iPhone. His parents immediately took him to the hospital. There he was diagnosed with renal deficiency, which was gradually deteriorating.

Moreover, police filed a case against the phony doctor and Liam. During investigation, it was revealed that the doctor, who paid Liam only $2000, had actually charged $18000 from the customer. Now Liam's doctors are trying to find a kidney donor to save him.

Give-and-Take Session

Like Liam, Bill Gates and Steve Jobs also had passion for gadgets. But they took a different path. Instead of buying such gadgets, they worked hard to make them.

While Liam's case of yielding to temptations is an extreme example, it is a common weakness among all animals, including human beings. Most animals have only a few basic temptations. For example a dog or cat can be lured with food, but not with an iPhone. Animals may be curious about an iPhone, but not interested in it.

Humans are evolved social animals. As a social animal, we enjoy many advantages of society. But it has some negative aspects too. And these negative aspects of the society impact some weak persons more. All children are not strong enough emotionally and mentally to handle the temptations. They are passing through a transition period. They are at an impressionable age. So they often become soft targets, particularly 'morally weak' children.

Most children know what is right and what is wrong. But very few have the wisdom to apply that knowledge. Many follow the wisdom of their parents and teachers to embrace a safe, secure and successful way of life. However, some children are not intelligent enough to avail this advantage.

But then, it's not that mentally weak children cannot become strong. Mahatma Gandhi, one of the most honest men of the 20th century, once stole a piece of gold from his brother and sold it. In his childhood, Gandhi was also addicted to smoking. But he realized his mistakes in time and later became a leader in the truest sense of the word. He won the freedom for his country with his intellect. He used honesty and nonviolence to win freedom for 400 million people without any war or bloodshed.

Points to Ponder

- Why Liam wanted an iPhone?
- Why Liam did not involve his parents or any friend in his deal?
- Liam knew the fact that selling a kidney is illegal. Why this fact could not discourage him?
- Why we can tempt animals with their primary needs like food? Can we always influence animals with food?
- Why most human beings have weakness for worldly things like car, mobile or iPad, which are not essential for them?
- Animals kill other animals for their food or safety, and many human beings also commit crime but rarely for their primary needs. Can we call ourselves more intelligent and developed than animals? Considering the criminal behavior of animals and humans, who are more humane?
- Why weak children often give in to unreasonable temptations? Can we blame their parents and teachers for their stupidity?

How do you tell right from wrong? Many years ago, Harry Fosdick developed a formula that helped him determine right from wrong. He called it 'six ways to tell right from wrong'. He suggested we test our potential actions against these six criteria:

The Common Sense Test – Are you simply being foolish? How would you judge someone else if they did the same thing?
"For in the same way you judge others, you will be judged, and with the measure you use, it will be measured to you." – Matthew 7:2

The Sportsmanship Test – Are you playing fair? How would you feel if someone else did the same thing to you? If it is not right for everyone, it is probably not right for anyone.
"Treat others the way you would want them to treat you." – Matthew 7:12

The Best Self-Test – Are you trying to be the best that you can be? Will it help you become a better person?
"Work hard at whatever you do." – Ecclesiastes 9:10

The Publicity Test – If everyone knew what you were doing, would you still do it? It is surprising how the light of public knowledge changes our perspective and our behavior.
"In the same way, let your light shine before men, that they may see your good deeds and praise your Father in heaven." – Matthew 5:16

The Most Admired Person Test – Would the person you most admired do this? If you told that person about it, would you feel proud or ashamed?
"Christ suffered for you, leaving you an example that you should follow in his steps." – 1 Peter 2:21

The Foresight Test – What can possibly go wrong? Could you live with the consequences?
"Do not brag about tomorrow! Each day brings its own surprises." – Proverbs 27:1

These six ways can help you to tell right from wrong. When you have important decisions to make, use this formula to choose wisely.

Remember, life is what you make it. Choice is yours. And remember your choices today will determine who you are tomorrow.

18. When Your Wish Comes True

Purpose of the Module: The aim of this story is to encourage children to make their choices responsibly and intelligently. While children are free to choose their hobbies, role models, etc., they should always follow a balanced approach and use their sense of right and wrong. And whenever in doubt, they must seek advice from elders.

Key Values: Appreciating Fantasy vs. Reality, Sense of Right and Wrong.
Supplementary Values: Obedience, Reasonableness, Self-restraint.
Life Skills: Self-discipline, Willpower.
Estimated Storytelling Time: 5 to 8 Minutes
Give-and-Take Session: 5 to 9 Minutes

Whitney was a seven-year-old girl. She was a good, bright girl, but had one very bad habit. She was a stubborn, copycat-type girl. And she was obsessed with Barbie dolls.

Whitney had a huge collection of Barbie dolls. She spent all her time playing with them. As soon as a new Barbie doll was released, she would buy it. She would even buy all the Barbie outfits and accessories. She would spend hours playing with them and dressing them. She loved to eat her food with them. She even used to put them to sleep before sleeping herself.

When Whitney turned eight, her obsession came to its peak. She wanted to become a Barbie doll herself so that she could talk to them. She wanted to play with her dolls. She started dressing up like her dolls.

One day, she asked her mother, "Can I become a Barbie doll?"

Her mother smiled and replied, "You are already a doll. Our princess doll."

She persisted, "But I am not a Barbie doll. I want to become one."

Her mother probed, "What would you do when you become one?"

She excitedly replied, "I will live with them in their home and talk to them day and night."

Her mother knew that Whitney was too stubborn to reason with. So she gently told her, "If you really want to be a Barbie doll then be a good girl for a fortnight. Don't be stubborn for 15 days. Impress God and he may grant your wish."

Whitney was so desperate to become a doll that she exactly followed her mother's instructions. And she became a very good girl indeed. She stopped arguing for anything.

After 14 days, God came near her and said, "You have been a very good girl Whitney. You may ask for whatever you want my child and it will be done for you."

Whitney bowed her head and said, "Dear God, I want to become a Barbie doll."

God said, "As you wish, so shall you be."

Like a shot, Whitney became a Barbie doll. She was very happy. She ran to her dolls and started talking with them. But they didn't reply. They didn't even look at her. She sat near them and tried hard to catch their attention. But the dolls sat motionless.

After some time, Whitney got bored. She felt stupid to talk to herself. So she wanted to tell her mother the whole story. But she was shocked to see her mother. Her mother looked like a giant. She tried hard to reach her but all she could reach was her lower legs. She tried hard to climb the couch on which her mother was sitting. The couch seemed like a big mountain. It took her half an hour to reach the armrest. She was out of breath by that time still she tried hard to call her mother. But her mother didn't hear her feeble voice. She tried shouting and everything but all her efforts went in vain.

By this time, she was very tired, very sleepy, and very hungry. So she went to the kitchen to get something to eat. Going to the kitchen was again an uphill task. When she finally reached the kitchen and tried to take one cookie from the plate, she realized that the cookie was about her own size. She could not lift it, not to speak of eating it. She was also feeling very thirsty. So she went to the coke bottle to take a few sips. She had to climb the coke bottle. When she reached the top, she opened it and tried to put her head into it. But before she could think about how to drink it, her arms gave up and she fell into the coke bottle. She screamed as she was drowning into it. She crazily prayed to God to help her.

Suddenly her bed sheets were pulled, and there stood her parents. They were trying to wake her up from her nightmare. She suddenly realized that it was just a nightmare. She hugged her parents and explained her dream. Her father kissed her and said, "What you considered to be a beautiful dream was actually a nightmare. I hope you have realized your mistake. Now you will behave in a responsible and sensible manner."

Whitney blurted a reply, "I will always follow you. God promise."

Her mother kissed her and said, "You should, till you come of age. It's good you understood now. Many children make mistakes in teenage and they don't realize before it's too late."

Give-and-Take Session

Kids always have dreams about what they want to be when they grow up. Today's small children want to become somebody like Superman or Batman, and girls want to be Superwoman or Cinderella. When they grow up a bit, children want to become just like their favorite movie or TV stars. Some children do everything in order to mimic these cool characters. They see the magazine covers of glamorous celebrities and try to mimic the look. They want to look great from head-to-toe like their favorite celebrity. Many children become unhappy and frustrated with themselves if they do not get the result they wanted. The formative years, particularly the pre-teen or teen years, can be a challenging time for anyone, with school pressures, anxieties about appearance and increasing independence.

Heroes aren't bad. Children learn a great deal by imitating positive heroes. Actually, we need more positive heroes to look up to. Part of being human is the ability to imagine other worlds, to fantasize. It's an important talent that brings about many others, including planning, lying, focusing and probing. But we should know how to keep fantasy distinct from reality. Psychologically, tweens and teens are most vulnerable to what they see in the media. They know the difference between fantasy and reality, but they lack the perspective. And the problem is that any fictional character can become an idol, and an obsession.

We all have something or someone we've become obsessed with at some point in our life. And many people don't even realize that they are obsessed with something or someone. An obsession often starts off innocently. First you like a person or a thing, than you begin to desire it, then you think you have to have it, and this put you in a position where you are constantly thinking about it and craving for it and then obsession hits you.

Obsession is unhealthy. It can lead you into depression, jealousy, envy, hatred, especially if you can't get the very thing you are obsessed with. And even if you get the thing, your obsession often causes you to experience big mood swings from brief periods of great joy to intense anxiety and depression. You begin to lose touch with the reality. And it can side track you from your life's planned journey.

It is not necessary that media exposure or fantasy stories are bad for children. They can be good for a range of intellectual skills, and for an imaginative and flexible engagement with the reality. The right way to deal with this issue is to ensure balance. The same way a nutritious diet helps promote healthy growth for kids' bodies, a balanced fiction diet promotes healthy growth for their minds.

Points to Ponder

- Ask yourself. Do I understand the difference between reality and media hype?
- Like all little girls, Whitney also used to like Barbie dolls. What's wrong in it?
- Why God didn't caution her about the dangers of becoming a doll?
- Why Whitney had such a scary nightmare?
- Children learn a great deal by imitating adults. Is it correct?
- Why children are more influenced by what they see in the media?
- Obsession with anything or any person is not healthy. And it can be dangerous. Do you agree?
- How we can have a healthy diet of fiction and media?
- The only healthy obsession you can have is one with yourself. Is it correct?

You can always take others advice to decide what really matters to you in life. But only you have to choose what is good for you. This freedom to choose carries with it the responsibility for your choices. So it is really important to choose your hobbies, role models, etc. intelligently.

Remember, you are unique, just like everyone else! So be yourself, be original, and be proud, because there is only one of you. Don't become a copy of anyone. Make up your mind to be the best of you; for God wants to bless the world through you.

May all your good wishes come true!

19. What If I Crawl

Purpose of the Module: This section attempts to make the students aware of the pitfalls of imitating or blindly copying others. They should be encouraged to find the correct path on their own instead of blindly following others. They should intelligently use their sense of discrimination between right and wrong while managing pressure from peers and media.

Key Values: Appreciating the Family Love, Managing Peer Pressure, Self-esteem.
Supplementary Values: Sense of Right and Wrong, Self-motivation.
Life Skills: Willpower, Independence, Self-discipline.
Estimated Storytelling Time: 6 to 8 Minutes
Give-and-Take Session: 6 to 10 Minutes

Jessica was a sweet 6-year-old girl. Last Sunday, she celebrated her little sister Jasmine's birthday. Jessica loved Jasmine and got along well with her, but sometimes she felt that her parents loved Jasmine more. They were always busy with her and gave her all their attention. Jessica often felt that she was being ignored.

Gradually she began to believe that now her parents loved only Jasmine. Before Jasmine was born, they used to really love her. Their affection towards her was not the same as it used to be. She felt a strange kind of loneliness in her own home. Her mother was always busy with Jasmine, as if she didn't even exist. All the time mother was busy doing one thing or another for Jasmine like feeding her or changing her clothes. Her parents played silly games with Jasmine. They never played with Jessica anymore. All these things made Jessica very sad and depressed. She wanted to win back her parents love, but didn't know how.

She observed that Jasmine would always do silly things like crawl around or make funny faces. Whenever Jasmine did something of this sort, her parents would say how cute she was and hugged and kissed her. So she decided that she would also behave like Jasmine to grab their attention.

First she started by small things like making faces like Jasmine. When that went unnoticed by her parents, she thought that it was time for drastic measures. She started imitating everything that Jasmine did. She started throwing childish tantrums, crying when she was hungry and even started to babble like Jasmine.

When her mother noticed all these changes, she got a bit concerned. And as they were taking dinner, Jasmine spilled some milk out of her mouth. Seeing this, Jessica also spilled her juice out of her mouth. Her mother got angry. She wanted to scold her, but decided that she would first talk to her husband about all this.

After dinner as all of them were getting ready to go to sleep, Jasmine wet her pants. Her parents started running around to get her nappy and baby powder. Then both her father and mother started to change it. Seeing this Jessica also wetted her pants. Her parents thought that she was ill. They decided to take her to the doctor the next day.

Next morning as they were going down for breakfast, Jasmine started crawling. Jessica also started crawling. Immediately her mother realized that Jessica was not ill. She understood what Jessica had been going through. She got tears in her eyes and was going to hug her when her husband stopped her and said, "No, first we should explain her that what she has been thinking is wrong. If you hug her now she will believe that this is the way to get attention. Then she may continue her babyish behavior. Let me talk to her first."

He sat beside Jessica and said, "Dear! You are very intelligent, and normally you take right decisions. But if you think that we love Jasmine more than we love you. You are wrong. We love both of you equally as both of you are our little angels. We treated you the same way when you were little. You even got better treatment than Jasmine as at that time we had to take care of only you. Now we have to take care of you and Jasmine both. You always got new toys when you were little but Jasmine got some of your old toys. You were our first child and we were very devoted to you. Even now we love you as much as we ever did. We give more attention to Jasmine because she is little and she needs it. You are my grown up princess. You are a good girl who knows how to take care of herself. Now stop being silly and start acting your age. Show mummy and daddy what a good girl you are. Be a responsible sister so that by watching you Jasmine also learns how she is supposed to behave when she grows up."

Trying to mask her embarrassment, Jessica stammered, "Sorry. I promise to be a good girl."

Her mother said, "Take it lightly. We all behave like copycats sometimes in our life. Even I started smoking when I was 19 copying other girls. As smoking is habit-forming, now you see my breathing and other health problems. I am still suffering because of that copycat behavior."

Her father said, "When I was in 10th grade, I bought a gun to teach a school bully a lesson in his own language. But fortunately, my mom caught my gun before I could do anything. I was saved. But that bully was not so lucky. Now he is in jail. He must be regretting his childish behavior in the school."

He then hugged her and her mother also came and kissed the top of her head. Jasmine also got up and sat in her lap.

Jessica realized her mistake and started laughing at her foolishness. She thanked God for giving her such lovely parents and such a lovely sister.

Give-and-Take Session

Little Jessica's case of trying to get attention by imitating her sister is not a rare one. We all knowingly or unknowingly imitate others. For example, we copy the clothes we see others wearing, we imitate our neighbors to maintain our status in the locality, and we want to buy the latest mobile just because our friends have bought it. Jessica's act was childlike. But when grownups imitate, it's childish.

While unconscious imitation is a universal phenomenon, real victims of this menace are children, particularly pre-teens and teenagers. They know the difference between fantasy and reality, but they lack the perspective to decide whether or not they are right. What's more, some of them can no longer be told how to behave or what to believe. They develop their own sense of what is right.

Many children play video games because their friends play. Some go to the mall or disco for the same reason. Others prefer to buy what their friends are buying (or what advertisers influenced them to buy). As always, businesses are good at making the most of our soft spots.

In this day and age of internet, children have access to material that is too advanced for them and could be quite harmful to their physical and mental health, but good for the financial health of businesses. Children watch a lot of television and are exposed to an awful lot of risky and violent behavior. Media pushes a 'machine-like' view of the world, treats children as objects and promotes unhealthy behaviors to them. Unfortunately, 'morally weak' children, who seek instant gratification of their desires, often become the soft target.

The unhealthy behaviors can be infectious among children. Students, whose friends smoke, drink or use drugs, for example, are more likely to show such behavior problems. Friends and media play a big role in negative destructive behaviors like teen runaways, substance use and self injurious behaviors like lying, violent outbursts and self-harm. These unhealthy behaviors are often fuelled by peer pressure and media.

The challenges of life can be overwhelming for students who often feel powerless to do anything about them. In addition to academic pressures, sports, and school activities, students also deal with pressures like, finding a sense of self, adjusting to growing up, and choosing a career path, among others.

But then, you can't ignore that school years are the best years of your life and set the stage for your future. So, it's important to identify your stress triggers and avoid unhealthy practices to ensure a healthy and successful transition to adulthood. Remember, the seeds of a successful transition to adulthood are planted in early years.

Points to Ponder

- Why Jessica was very sad and depressed?
- Who was responsible for Jessica's sadness and depression?
- What would you do if you feel your parents treat your brother or sister better than you?
- Do children engaging in risky behaviors face regretful outcomes as adults? Why?
- How could Jessica's father consider him lucky when his mother scolded him very badly for buying a gun?
- Health warnings regarding smoking are well known and health messages on cigarette packages deliver important information directly to smokers. Why Jessica's mother disregarded these warnings? Why she continues to suffer even after realizing her folly?
- What is the relationship between positive adolescent behaviors and adult outcomes?

Watching other successful people and trying to do what they do is a good way to learn things. Attempting to be someone you're not can be good when it involves improving academic, sport, and other positive skills. It can be very destructive when you're trying to 'be like' someone else just to have their appearance and popularity.

Students should try to develop a sense of identity, and feel secure in that identity. The idea is that if you try to be someone else, you'll not feel too good. Developing your self-esteem is probably the best antidote to deal with the present-day negative influences.

"Give all your worries and cares to God, for he cares about you" ~1 Peter 5:7

20. The No-Gadget Trip

Purpose of the Module: This module aims to encourage children to appreciate how family members care for each other. They should understand the importance of family love and support, and try to maintain a right balance between their needs and the needs of their family. They should also be encouraged to spend more time in the natural environment and use their tech devices responsibly.

Key Values: Appreciating the Family Love, Compassion.
Supplementary Values: Sharing, Caring, Giving.
Life Skills: Balance, Self-control, Organizing.
Estimated Storytelling Time: 6 to 8 Minutes
Give-and-Take Session: 6 to 10 Minutes

Peter was excited about his no-gadget camping trip. The science teacher was taking his class on a camping trip to the city's outskirts. Peter was busy packing his things while his mother was busy preparing some snacks for him to take along.

Peter's 3-year-old little sister, Lucy asked her mother why Peter was packing his things. When her mother explained her about the no-gadget trip, she asked, "So brother will be staying without electricity? Then how will he watch TV?"

Her mother smiled and replied, "He won't be watching TV or going online this weekend."

Then Lucy wondered aloud, "Won't he get bored?"

Mother said, "Let's see."

Lucy thought for a moment then suddenly ran to her room.

After some time, she came to Peter's room and started keeping a few things in his suitcase. When he asked what they were, she replied, "It's a surprise. Check it yourself when you reach the camp."

After keeping the things, she instructed him, "In the left side of your suitcase, I have kept your playthings and on the right, there is a note. Read the note first then take out the things."

Students had to walk three miles to reach the camp site, as there was no motorable road in the forest. They spent first day in making arrangements for their stay and getting used to their surroundings. On the next day while all his friends were discussing pros and cons of gadgets in our lives, Peter took out the things, which Lucy had kept in his suitcase. He was surprised to see a tiny teddy bear, an old Barbie bracelet, a toy gun and three empty chocolate wrappers there. His friends made fun of him as he had brought a teddy bear along with him. He got angry and threw the junk out.

After the trip when Peter returned home, Lucy came running to him and asked, "Did you like my presents? Did you read my note? I hope Mr. Teddy played with you when you were getting bored. He always plays with me. And you saw those three chocolate wrappers? One was given to me by mommy, one by daddy and one by you. They always make me smile when I look at them. That bracelet, which grandma gave me, keeps me safe from goblins. And did you use the gun on wild animals?" She then demanded her stuff back.

Peter looked at her uneasily, trying to come up with an excuse that would satisfy her. He was finding it hard to control his emotions. With some efforts, he controlled himself. Then he told her that he had kept them in his friend's bag, as there was no space in his bag. He also assured her that he would bring them back tomorrow.

Lucy asked, "You didn't lose them, did you. I need Mr. Teddy when I sleep."

Trying to mask his expressions, which he seemed to do very well,

Peter promised her that he would definitely get them back tomorrow.

That night, after Lucy slept, he took out her note and read it. Written in big alphabets were the words 'I luv you Peter. Take care.'

Immediately, Peter went to his father's room and told him the whole story. With tears in his eyes he admitted, "I didn't realize that those were her treasures that she has given to me out of love so that I don't get bored. Please help me to get them back dad."

Without delay, Peter and his father went to the campsite with searchlights. After an hour of searching, they finally found Lucy's things and brought them back. Peter washed everything including Mr. Teddy as the things got spoiled due to dirt.

While doing all this, Peter realized the importance of family love in life. He was touched by the gesture of affection his little sister showed despite her years.

Give-and-Take Session

We are social beings who live in the community with other social beings. Our family is our first community, our first school, our first playground– In fact it is the first step in the socialization process. The family is the foundation of any individual's ability to love and accept love.

Our first experience with love is the love shared between parents and children. The emotional foundation laid by our family determines how we love, live and greet life. It shapes our view of the world; it determines our success. And it is where we seek refuge when life seems overwhelming.

The family is meant to be a school in which human beings learn about sharing, caring and giving. With the onslaught of tech gadgets, people are not getting enough time for their family members. Nowadays tech-obsessed children are more preoccupied with their life and their gadgets. Their preoccupation with the self is not allowing them to make the most of nurturing atmosphere of family. The most important element of a family is love. And it is difficult to figure out the long term effect of the digital world on this most important element.

Many parents are really concerned about the impact of cyber-culture and the stress that comes with it. The new technology has changed the way children connect with others. It makes them both more social and unsocial. They are more social because they are always reachable on mobile or internet, but this also means multitasking most of the time. Multitasking makes them divided and not totally present which makes them somewhat unsocial.

The technology has fundamentally changed the ways in which people, including young children, relate to each other, both individually and collectively. Many experts have begun to wonder whether this is a good thing or not. In favor of technology, there is an argument that technology is preparing children for the future. Children need the tech advantage to succeed in life, especially when most of the jobs in the market are technology related.

But then, some experts argue that children who use technology are becoming socially deficient, ungrateful and unhealthy. Children need a natural learning environment and real-world experiences. Technology can promote style over substance, but human contact really matters. Children need to be comforted, cuddled and groomed. They need personal attention and tender loving care.

Points to Ponder
(It is not necessary for students to answer the questions or participate in discussion. They are just required to ponder over them. So, after every question or statement, a brief pause is recommended so as to allow their subconscious mind to absorb the desired values.)

- Why the science teacher planned a no-gadget trip?
- Why there was no road in the forest?
- Honesty is the best policy. But Peter lied to his sister. Do you think he was right in what he did? Why?

- Think a while about your family members. Do you love them all equally?
- Can you imagine a world without family love?
- Children are being overexposed to computers and other tech devices. Think a while about the pros and cons of tech gadgets.
- Can you imagine a world without technology?
- Do you believe students exposed to technology are unsociable?
- Do you believe students exposed to technology are more prone to health risks such as obesity and sleep problems?
- Steve Jobs wanted to embrace a natural lifestyle. When he was 18, he went to India for this purpose. But his experience was disappointing due to some black sheep. Do you think he reversed gears and embraced technology to take revenge by developing so many tech devices?
- Do you have any other comment about the future of children and technology?

In today's constantly connected world, children are never totally alone. Is it more social or antisocial? It is a really interesting riddle. But we have no definite answers in such a rapidly changing world. It's not possible to accurately foresee how technology will affect today's children particularly when we can barely imagine the technology they'll be using in the future. No one really knows how this constant use of high-tech gadgets will affect today's children. We'll have to wait and see!

Today's children should realize that this is the first generation of children who have unrestricted access to the internet and mobile, and it is still too soon to say that technology is definitively good or bad for them. So, like anything else in life, there needs to be a balance between the risks of having too much and the risks of having too little exposure to the technology. And moderation is the key word to use it in a healthy way.

21. The Art of Giving

Purpose of the Module: It attempts to make the students aware of growing disparities and inequalities between the rich and poor. And encourage them to think how they can make a difference in a responsible way to help the underprivileged sections of the society. It also seeks to emphasize again the importance of being honest and acting with integrity.

Key Values: Sense of Social Responsibility, Integrity.
Supplementary Values: Honesty, Humanism, Kindness, Concern for Others, Equality.
Life Skills: Caring, Sharing, Giving.
Estimated Storytelling Time: 5 to 7 Minutes
Give-and-Take Session: 6 to 8 Minutes

Mr. Michael was a socially responsible trader of grains. His business was flourishing because he sold good quality grains at a very reasonable price. Because of his honest trade practices and good reputation, he became the biggest trader in the state. This further encouraged him to supply grains to the poor and needy people at a discounted price. He also started offering credit facility or free grains to very poor people who could not afford two square meals. His competitors were annoyed. His low profit policy was affecting their business.

Michael was getting old. He often wondered who would take charge of the business after him. He was worried about the continuity of his business, particularly his fair price policy for the people. He had only one son who was like other corrupt traders. In almost everything, his son, Michael Jr. was the opposite of his father. While Michael believed in simple living and high thinking, Michael Jr. was alcoholic and drug addict. There were rumors that Michael Jr. had many other vices too. Unlike his father, he wanted to make quick money by hook or crook. He was in favor of selling adulterated grains at good profit like other traders.

Michael was sure that if he gave charge of his business to his son, business would be ruined in no time. Moreover, his son would indulge more in his bad habits. He was also concerned about the poor people dependent on his subsidized grains. He was desperately searching for an honest employee so as to ensure continuity of his business. He wanted his business to continue to flourish as well as benefit people of his state forever.

Michael shared his thoughts with his close friends. He asked for their advice so that he could identify the most honest person among his employees. One wise friend suggested that while giving the Christmas bonus envelopes, he should give everyone double the amount than their entitlement. And the employee, who would return the extra money, should be considered for the top job if he was caring and sympathetic towards the people. Michael followed his advice. He declared one month's salary as Christmas bonus, but filled all the bonus envelopes with two months' salary.

All his employees knew that they had received much more money by mistake, but they kept quiet. Paul was an honest and hard-working manager in the Michael's company. He had recently lost some money in the stock market. He thought for a while on what he should do. He was a bit confused because of his urgent need for money. Then he wondered what would be the right thing to do. For an honest person like Paul, the answer was obvious.

Paul went to Mr. Michael's office and returned the extra money. Michael, who was aware of Paul's recent losses, was surprised to see that Paul returned the extra bonus even though he desperately needed it. His other employees, who were rich and didn't need extra money, knowingly kept the undue money.

He asked Paul to sit and said, "I'm a bit worried. This year our profit is not good. What's more, our per-unit profit margin is falling due to discounts to the poor people. I'm afraid we may not be able to give increments to the staff in January. We have to discontinue the subsidy to the poor if we have to raise the salaries. What is your opinion?"

Paul immediately replied, "We should not discontinue discounts to the poor. They are dependent on us. Staff can always get raise in future when we make good profit."

Michael interrupted, "When our profit margin is continuously falling, how we can make good profit in future."

Paul smiled and said, "Our per-unit profit may continue to fall because of very low prices, but our sales volume will grow substantially because of reasonable prices. And it will ultimately increase our profits. Besides, we get an inner satisfaction by helping the needy sections of the society. And that is priceless."

Michael was pleased with his reply. He smiled and informed Paul about his plan. After a few days, Paul succeeded Michael as the head of the business.

Give-and-Take Session

Many of you might have heard the story of Charles 'Chuck' Colson who was not a socially responsible person earlier in his life, but later he became one of the best social engineers of his time.

Charles Colson was President Nixon's hatchet man-in-chief during the Watergate years. As President's special counsel, Colson enjoyed power and prestige. He had his own office in the White House. But after Watergate scandal, he was sent to prison because of his dishonest and socially unacceptable conduct.

Colson went from the pinnacle of political power to the humiliation of becoming a convicted crook. While in prison, Colson experienced a religious conversion that changed his life. This experience changed him radically; he realized his folly and then became a socially responsible person.

After serving time in prison, Colson forged a new career as a respected author and speaker to share his message with others. He received 15 honorary doctorates and many prestigious awards. He donated all his earnings including prize money, speaking fees and royalties. He will be remembered as a person who had a complete turnaround in his life. Here is an edited excerpt from one of his final lectures wherein he summarized his views on the root causes of the cultural problems threatening our society. "I discovered early on that the reasons the prisons were being filled wasn't all the sociological theories about crime that we hear generally, it was the lack of moral training during the morally formative years. We are raising a generation that lacks male role models. The family has broken down. These kids aren't learning character."

Points to Ponder

- Why Michael was known as a socially responsible trader?
- How he became the biggest trader in the state?
- Why his competitors were not happy?
- Why was Michael reluctant to hand over the charge to his son?
- What was the dilemma that Paul was facing while thinking to return the extra money?
- How did the Paul's honest act benefit him?
- Before his prison term, Charles Colson was a powerful, rich man. Can we compare Michael or his son to young Colson before his prison stint?
- Can we compare Charles Colson after he had a complete turnaround in his life to Michael? How?
- We hear a lot about human progress. We also hear that the rich are becoming richer and the poor are becoming poorer. Does human progress means a situation in which the rich become richer and the poor, poorer?
- We rarely hear about human regress, a situation where the gap between the rich and the poor increases. Why leaders talk more about human progress and less about human regress?
- If we are progressing, then why the gap between the rich and the poor is widening?
- Do we need honest politicians who really try to bring equality in the world?

- Our character is what we do when we think no one is looking. Do you agree with it? Do you follow it?

Henry David Thoreau beautifully summarized the importance of goodness by saying, "Goodness is the only investment that never fails."

If you do good to others, it will never fail. If you are good to people, it will always come back to you with interest. It's wiser to invest in good deeds to attract happiness and positive energy.

Always remember the golden rule. "Do unto others as you would have them do unto you." Doing good to others is an important aspect of life. By being good, you can expect its positive outcomes. It always pays to be good. It is said that when you do good to others, you are best to yourself. And honesty is an important aspect of goodness.

When you are honest, you build strength of character that will allow you to succeed in life. And you will be blessed with self-respect and peace of mind. Therefore, you all should try to be honest in your life and with your life.

Remember, humanity is one and this small earth is our only home. If we are to protect this home of ours, each of us needs to have a sense of responsibility and a sincere concern for the welfare of others. Only then we can make our planet more human and humane.

Try to be the best you can be. You are sure to be happy and successful in life. May all the good you do come back to you, with interest.

22. Every Dog Has Its Way

Purpose of the Module: The aim of this section is to familiarize students with the risks of substance abuse, and how a person enslaved by drugs can behave in a very weird fashion. Students should be made to understand that an addict is driven by cravings that are overwhelming, resulting in loss of values, integrity and self-respect. They should also appreciate that honesty means much more than not telling lies; it is a sincere devotion to truthfulness in letter and spirit.

Key Values: Honesty, Avoiding Drugs.
Supplementary Values: Kindness to Animals, Abstinence.
Life Skills: Integrity, Self-awareness.
Estimated Storytelling Time: 4 to 6 Minutes
Give-and-Take Session: 6 to 9 Minutes

Crooked Draco was a habitual drug abuser. It was not known whether he became crooked because of his drug habit or he became drug addict because of his crookedness. It was like cracking the mystery of which came first, the chicken or the egg.

Once, Draco stole a German Shepherd dog from a priest's home. He planned to sell the dog to make some quick bucks, as he desperately wanted to buy heroin. While he was going to the market after hiding the dog in his home, in a very rare appearance his conscience struck him. He felt a bit bad about stealing that too from a priest's house. He thought a lot about it. The more he thought the more confused he became. The dilemma was overwhelming for a straightforward crooked man. However, he finally made up his mind to accept his crime and tell the truth to the priest. He decided to go to the church and confess his sin.

While his conscience was pricking him badly for the sinful act, his urge for drugs was trying to control his conscience. However, he went to the church and knelt in the confession box. Bowing his head, he said, "Father, I stole a dog today."

The priest politely posed a question, "Why did you steal it? That is not a good thing."

Draco sheepishly replied, "I have no money. I wanted to sell it and buy some medicines." Before the priest could say anything, he again said, "Do you want to keep the dog?"

The priest sympathetically replied, "No, you should take it back to its rightful owner. And take your medicines from the church's account"

Draco blurted a reply, "I tried to return it but he refused to take it."

The priest thought for a while and then advised him, "Well in that case, you can keep the dog. And take good care of it"

Draco bowed his head and gratefully said, "Thank you, father."

When the priest returned home, he did not find his German Shepherd. The dog was missing. He was upset and sad because he really loved his dog. He prayed for the well being of his dog.

Meanwhile, Draco went to the market and sold the dog to a rich businessman. He took 10% advance from the buyer and pledged his expensive but stolen watch as security till he delivered the dog. He immediately bought heroin from the advance money. After having heroin, he was on a high.

Draco happily went back to his home to get the dog. As he was taking the dog to the market, he casually told the dog, "I tried to return you to your master but he refused to take you."

Suddenly the dog bit him on his face. Draco panicked and pleaded, "I have found a new owner for you. He will take good care of you." Then the dog bit him again on his leg.

As Draco was crying in pain, the dog barked twice as if telling him one bite for giving the wrong impression to my master and the second for stealing, and ran away to the priest's home.

The crooked man was drug abuser as well as dishonest. Perhaps, his drug addiction and dishonesty were feeding on each other. He not only stole the dog but also lied to the priest. Draco did not tell the priest that he was talking about the priest's dog, and he never actually asked the priest whether he wanted his German Shepherd back. As he was talking to the dog, the dog bit him first on his face because he lied when he said that the owner of the dog has refused to take him back. The dog again bit him when he said that I had found a new home for you as he was only making money by an act of stealing.

Give-and-Take Session

Draco was a drug addict. His drug habit forced him to engage in morally wrong activities. His drug habit made him lie. But many of us do morally incorrect things unnecessarily. Some examples are: children who lie or hide facts from their parents, students who use unfair means to complete their assignments, businesses that use unethical means to gain an unfair advantage over rivals.

Lies come from fear, anxiety and temptations. And it is not that just common people like you and me give in to temptations. Many political and business leaders behave unethically for their selfish motives. Some historians allege that American presidents like Nixon, Clinton and Bush misrepresented facts in their political career. Some like Clinton acknowledge wrongdoing, repent, and make amends to become better people. Saying 'sorry' is a courageous act and takes strength. Clinton not only survived, but prospered as he finished his term with the highest end-of-office approval rating of any U.S. president since World War II. It was a remarkable feat considering that at one time, his impeachment issue rocked, shocked and rolled his country.

Some people like Nixon are not wise enough to realize their folly in time and suffer the consequences. Saying 'sorry' is tough and accepting mistakes is even tougher. But it is necessary for a wrongdoer, as it shows that he is trying to change. A sincere apology in itself can be enough to soothe wounds and make a new beginning.

Points to Ponder
(Remind the students the words of Robert Louis Stevenson: "In each of us, two natures are at war – the good and the evil. All our lives the fight goes on between them, and one of them must conquer. But in our own hands lies the power to choose – what we want most to be we are." And then encourage them to imagine a white angel and a red devil sitting on their shoulders and debating between themselves. Also remind them that the devil represents temptation and the angel represents conscience.)

- Why Draco stole the priest's dog?
- Why Draco's conscience pricked him?
- How Draco confessed his mistake? Was it right on his part?
- What the dog was trying to say when it barked twice?
- How dogs helped prehistoric men?
- Over the years, dogs learned many things from humans, like yawning which is typically a copycat behavior, not common to its species. Do you know anything humans have learned from dogs?
- Drug addiction is not a bad habit. It is not a weakness. Drug addiction is a disease. Do you agree?
- Why drug addiction is also known as white plague? Why bad habits are hard to break?
- Drug addiction is an equal opportunity destroyer and devastator. Do you agree? Why?
- Not all lies are bad. Your comments?
- Honesty means never bending the truth. Do you agree?

We know that dogs are men's original best friends forever. Now scientists say that the smartest thing humans ever did was to choose the dog as loyal companion. This move tipped the balance against the now-extinct Neanderthals, a human like species who had been dominating large parts of earth for a quarter of a million years. Neanderthals looked much like modern humans, but were generally shorter and much more heavily built. They were more powerful and much stronger, particularly in the arms and hands.

Dogs made primitive man's life so much easier that he could conquer the world, unlike his dog-less Neanderthals who became extinct 30,000 years ago. The man and the dog, the worrier and the worry-free, were perfect companion to rule the world. Dogs have learnt a lot from human association. Dogs often understand what we say, but after all the scientific advances and Google translators and interpreters, we are not good enough to understand what dogs say. What's more, such a long association was not enough for us to follow the good qualities of dogs such as loyalty, devotion and unconditional love.

I conclude with the words of Roger Caras: "Dogs have given us their absolute all. We are the center of their universe. We are the focus of their love and faith and trust. They serve us in return for scraps. It is without a doubt the best deal man has ever made."

23. Friend or Frenemy

Purpose of the Module: In this module we revisit a value that the children are familiar with. But it is important to remind them that friendship is about trustworthiness, sharing and cooperation. It is about who we are, not what we have. It is about love, loyalty, and most of all fun. Children should also be reminded that false friends are worse than bitter enemies. Because it is easier to deal with someone who you know from the start is not on your side than someone who you thought was a friend but is really not.

Key Values: Friendship, Integrity.
Supplementary Values: Justice, Cooperation, Respect for the Environment, Sharing.
Life Skills: Perseverance, Integrity, Hard Work.
Estimated Storytelling Time: 6 to 8 Minutes
Give-and-Take Session: 5 to 10 Minutes

Bill and Steve were best friends since kindergarten. They were in the same class. They have lived next door to each other since birth. No one could separate them. As if they were long lost brothers who finally found each other. Their parents also knew each other.

Steve had a garden in front of his home. It was lovely and had various trees. The trees bore delicious fruits. Steve always shared the fruits with Bill and his family. Since no one bothered about the garden, the trees gradually became dull and pale. They no longer produced delicious fruits.

Steve was not happy with his shabby garden. He informed Bill about their plan and said, "I am fed up of this garden now. It's simply useless. My father is planning to convert it into a garage and storehouse like the one you have in front of your home."

Bill thought for a while and then suggested, "Why don't we ask our parents to exchange our land? You can have the garage and storehouse, and I can have the garden."

Steve asked in disbelief, "My garden is pretty useless and ugly. Do you really want it?

Bill said, "Yes. I love nature."

Steve replied, "If you insist, I will talk to dad tonight."

Their parents agreed, and they swapped each other's land. While Bill was looking forward to having his own garden, Steve was happy to get a garage to park his car. Bill wanted to make the garden as beautiful as it was a few years ago. He nurtured it. Every day, he watered the plants and trimmed the flowerbeds. He spent his whole weekends plucking out the weeds, etc. from the garden and paving the paths with stones.

His hard work paid off. In the next season, the trees were again laden with good quality fruits. Bill and his family were very happy. Bill took some fruits to Steve's home and told him how happy he was to revive the garden. Steve congratulated him and praised his hard work and passion for the nature.

That evening, Steve's father was shocked to see such good quality fruits. He regretted his decision to sell the land. He started scheming to get back the land. He made a cunning plan. He decided to talk to Bill's father the next morning, as he believed that he was the original and real owner of the trees. He had sowed the seeds from which his friend was reaping the benefits.

Next morning, Steve's father went to Bill's house and demanded all those fruits or payment to compensate for all the fruits. Bill's father was shocked to hear such a weird thing from his friend. After a while he replied that he had bought the land and the trees were part of the deal. They had an argument over who was the owner of trees. They could not resolve it. So they decided that the matter should be settled in the court.

Steve and Bill met next morning, both were apprehensive about their friendship. Steve said, "Listen whatever happened between our fathers is none of our business. It's their mistake that they value materialistic things more than their friendship."

Bill replied, "You are right. Whatever the outcome may be we will always remain best of friends." Both of them went home happily that day. They were proud of their friendship.

Next week, their fathers went to the court. Steve's father told the judge, "I sold him the land, not the trees. I sowed the seeds. Now he is eating all the fruits as if he is the owner."

Bill's father countered, "I bought the land from him. At that time, he didn't say anything about the trees. Now he is getting jealous seeing how the trees have grown so well. They grew because of my hard work not his."

The judge studied the case carefully. Then he straightened self-importantly in his chair and said to Steve's father, "You are right. I agree with your point. You sold him the land not the trees. But, you are keeping your property on his land and not even paying him rent. You need to pay him rent or take away your trees today itself. But make sure that while you are taking your trees away, you don't damage his land. The soil should not be affected in any way. Take just your trees without leaving a mark on the land."

Steve's father was stunned to hear this. He was simply knocked for six because of this. He had no option but to take back his appeal. After a small lecture from the judge, both of them realized their foolishness.

While Bill and Steve heaved a sigh of relief, their parents decided that they should learn from them. They were very proud of their children for the maturity shown by them. They decided to share the fruits, just like true friends should.

Later Bill Jobs and Steve Gates became very big and busy businessmen. Yet they would meet every Sunday morning to discuss what they were doing and how they could do it better. And in the evening, both friends planted trees, the fruits of which would be collected by future generations.

Give-and-Take Session

Friendship is a feeling of love and affection of one person for another. True friendship is built on trust and mutual support. Your real friend is always there to help you and expects the same from you. Friends enjoy the company of each other, and sometimes are emotionally closer to each other than with their own relatives.

A true friend makes you happy, can criticize without hurting and is bold to tell the truth. A true friend never exploits. A true friend is also one who pushes us to be a better version of who we are. Good friends exercise good influence. Your best friend is the one who brings out the best in you.

But then, there are many fair-weather friends. And very often some phonies pretend to be friends. They could be more dangerous than enemies. Why a dog is called man's best friend?

A dog cannot pretend to be a friend. It can't be a frenemy (A frenemy is an enemy disguised as a friend). Its affection, loyalty and devotion are amazing. A dog wants no more than to be with its friend and see joy in that friend's eyes. A dog loves its friend whether he is rich or poor, sick or well, busy or free, dead or alive. A dog will wait loyally for its friend for days, weeks, months. The best example is the true story of Hachiko, the dog who waited for his master at the exact same spot where he left him for ten years until its death. (*If practical, narrate the true tale of Hachiko, a Japanese Akita dog that became a national icon.*)

Points to Ponder

- Why Steve's father wanted his trees back? When judge allowed him to take his trees, why he changed his mind?

- Once Bill and Steve had a fight over a petty matter and stopped talking to each other. The Bulky Bully invited Bill to join his group and offered to teach Steve a dirty lesson. Do you think Bill should accept the offer? Why?
- Sometimes even good friends have fights and disagreements, but they apologize and forgive each other. Do you agree?
- A true friend knows your weakness but he'll emphasize your strong qualities.
- A true friend knows all your fears and worries but he'll try to build your confidence.
- A true friend recognizes your mistakes and weaknesses but he'll make you aware of your possibilities.
- A true friend is the most precious gift that you can receive in your life.
- Friends can influence each other, both in a positive way and in a negative way.
- As we grow and change, our interests, goals, and desires change. Is it reasonable to assume that our friends would change as a result?
- False friends are worse than bitter enemies. What does it mean?
- A dog cannot pretend to be a friend, and it can't be a frenemy. That's why a dog is always better than a bad friend. Do you agree?

Friendship is important in all phases of our life. It takes time to make a good friend, but it is worth the effort as having a confident can help you in many ways. Good friends are like gems, precious and rare. False friends are like leaves, found everywhere. A good friend is hard to find, hard to lose, and really hard to forget.

Remember, friends are God's way of taking good care of us.

24. Frog In A Well

Purpose of the Module: This section is intended to sensitize students about the under-privileged and help them understand the importance of being socially responsible. Students should appreciate that those who believe in simple living are better placed to succeed in life. They should recognize that materialistic factors – like their parents' status, or what they have, or how they enjoy life – will not determine their destiny.

Key Values: Humility, Simple Living.
Supplementary Values: Self-restraint, Managing Peer Pressure, Good Manners.
Life Skills: Willpower, Self-control, General Knowledge, Thriftiness.
Estimated Storytelling Time: 5 to 7 Minutes
Give-and-Take Session: 5 to 8 Minutes

Twelve-year-old Zac was a bright student. He always got good grades. His father was a rich stockbroker who invested his wealth as well as his client's money in the stock market. After making good money in the stock market, he gradually became overconfident and diverted his money to more speculative and riskier investments.

After the worldwide recession, he lost all the money invested in the shares. And he had to repay his client's money. He sold his mansion, yacht, Ferrari, Rolls Royce and other valuables to pay off his debts. After clearing all his debts, he and his family moved to a small two-room apartment, and he got a job in another stock brokerage firm. Though he was not earning well, he wanted his son to get good education. So, he got his son admitted to a good school.

Zac was happy to be in a good school. He made new friends. His friends often went to movies, parties, shopping, etc. but he always avoided. Knowing his family's financial situation, he never went out with them. His friends always invited him to join them but he politely refused every time. Finally, they were fed up of asking him daily. They thought that instead of asking him they should tease him to force him to join them. They started calling him 'Frog In A Well' or FIAW. Whenever they got a chance, they would call him by his new nickname, i.e., FIAW. But still he never went with them. Gradually, they started to enjoy teasing him and did that daily. They always teased him by telling the things like how amazing the movie was or how much they enjoyed at the Mall. He didn't seem to mind them much.

Before the summer holidays, they all made plans and discussed their plans with each other. Most of them were going to foreign countries for the holidays. They asked Zac about his summer plans. When Zac told them that he won't be going anywhere, they mockingly said, "Oh sorry! We asked you. We should have known that the FIAW doesn't come out of its well."

Zac spent most of the summer holidays reading new books. When the school reopened, everyone talked about how great their outings were. During the break, they all described their trips and asked Zac, "Hey FIAW what did you do? Took rounds of your well?" The class teacher who was passing by heard all this. She felt sorry for Zac, as she knew Zac's story. She was also aware that Zac was a sensitive, bright boy.

After recess, the teacher told the class that today there would be a test on general knowledge. Since the test was about places in the world, it was titled 'let's find our FIAW rank'. Everyone laughed and told Zac, "You are sure to top this one. Most of us will probably get a place at the bottom."

The next day the results were announced. Students were shocked to find that they all got higher rankings than Zac. In fact, Zac was on the last of FIAW index, i.e., he got the best grade. Most students, who were proud travelers, could not answer basic questions about places, history, cultures, etc. But Zac, who never went out, answered all the questions correctly.

The teacher gave everyone their answer sheets and explained, "Students we all are FIAW. Even I am a FIAW. Considering the vast knowledge pool, it is impossible for anyone not be a FIAW. The world is so vast that it is impossible for anyone to know all about it. We have the world and then the universe. Has anyone ever traveled the entire universe? Can anyone compare the size of earth and universe? Can anyone tell me how many times universe is bigger than earth?"

No student replied. They knew that the earth was very small as compared to other stars, and universe contained countless stars.

The teacher stared at the students for a while and then said, "While we all are FIAW, the only difference is how much is the size of our well. That means how much we know about the things that matter in life. That is what ultimately matters. Zac is a very bright student. That is why his well is the biggest among you all. You should all learn from Zac and try to expand your knowledge and become a frog of a really big well."

Students realized their mistake and apologized to Zac. He forgave them and they all became good friends.

Give-and-Take Session

In any society, some people are rich and others are poor. And rich people don't have the exclusive right to success. In fact, no one has monopoly over success.

How you spend your parent's wealth doesn't define your success. Success cannot be measured in terms of wealth. How you spend your time is a better indicator of your destiny.

Your status is not defined by what you have or where you go. It is defined by what you do. You need to define yourself not by what you have, but by your actions, and by what you achieve. While Zac's friends were having fun, Zac was working hard to improve his knowledge. And in the ultimate analysis of life, Zac would be a winner because he used his time on productive things. He would become a stronger person because of his abstinence and a simple lifestyle. Simple living is good not just for your academic performance, but also for your health – physical and emotional.

Even for persons who measure success in terms of wealth, it is worth noting that most of the top positions in the richest persons list are occupied by people who come from humble backgrounds, like Zac. But they achieved pinnacle of success with their sheer determination and hard work. Like Zac, such achievers are not concerned about what their peers say or do. They know what they are doing. They just continue their success march. And the good thing is that the secret of their success is no secret at all. It is their discipline and diligence, dedication and determination.

One such example was Charles Steinmetz, a German immigrant who was almost a dwarf, with a frail body and poor eyesight. Immigration authorities were reluctant to admit Steinmetz into the USA. His distorted body, poverty, and lack of resources led officials to believe that he was likely to become a liability for the state. When he was finally allowed to enter the country, Steinmetz had ten dollars, had no job prospects, and could not speak English.

Later Steinmetz invented an alternating current motor that was responsible for the electrification of world. He was immediately acclaimed a genius. Just to get Steinmetz, General Electric bought the company he worked for. But he preferred to stay with the employer who had given him his first job. A total of 195 patents were registered in his name. Despite the spectacular contributions he made to science and their immense potential to benefit the society, he remained throughout his life a man of exceptional humility.

You are aware that Abraham Lincoln is considered America's greatest president. And Benjamin Franklin is considered one of the greatest minds. Lincoln and Franklin also rose from very humble beginnings. But humility was their greatest virtue throughout their life.

Points to Ponder

- Why Zac's father had to sell his mansion?
- Why Zac would not go with his friends on fun trips?
- Why Zac's friends started teasing him. Why they used to call him FIAW?
- What Zac did in his summer holidays?
- Why GE wanted to buy Steinmetz's company?
- Why most top positions in the richest persons list are usually occupied by people who come from humble backgrounds?
- Humility involves genuinely understanding a situation/person before formulating your views. Do you agree?
- Why really successful people are always humble?

How you define happiness is very important. Some students have the wrong idea of what constitutes happiness. It is not attained through self-gratification but through dedication to a worthy purpose. People who don't appreciate the right definition of happiness feel less satisfied with their lives.

Seeking happiness through entertainment is important, but it is not life. And it is important not to let it get ahead of other important aspects of life. Remember, Ecclesiastes 3:1 says, "There is a time for everything and a season for every activity under heaven."

25. The True Friend

Purpose of the module: This story is planned to sensitize students about the evils of racism and the importance of tolerance. The objective is to teach students not to show prejudice based on others' physical attributes. Students should know that racism is an unfortunate part of our society, but there is no room for hatred in the school. Each student should appreciate that racism is against moral vision of life, and nobody is inferior or superior by birth.

Key Values: Tolerance, Equality.
Supplementary Values: Humanism, Dignity of the Individual, Respect for Others, Cooperation.
Life Skills: Fairness, Friendship, Good Manners.
Estimated Storytelling Time: 6 to 8 Minutes
Give-and-Take Session: 7 to 12 Minutes

Abigail was in the 7th grade. She and her family had just migrated from Africa. She was a bright girl who loved to help everyone. She was very excited while going to her new school for the first time. She was looking forward to new learning experiences and making new friends.

The teacher welcomed her warmly and introduced her to the class. She made Abigail sit in the first row with Katie. Abigail said Hi to Katie and introduced herself. Katie didn't reply. Abigail thought that maybe she was scared to speak in the presence of the teacher. Like Katie, she also focused on the topic for the rest of the period.

As soon as the teacher left, Katie picked up her things and went away without saying anything to Abigail. Abigail was a bit hurt. She wondered what she had done to offend Katie. She then decided to go and sit in the third row with a girl who was sitting alone. She went there and sweetly said, "May I sit here with you?"

The girl irritatingly retorted, "You may sit here but not with me. There is no way in this world that I will sit with someone like you."

Then she went away with her books. Abigail was deeply hurt and humiliated. She tried to control her tears and immersed herself in her books. Few boys started making fun of her curly hair. She tried to block their voices from her mind.

Katniss was watching all this from her seat. She was an intelligent girl who was selected from the class for the foreign exchange program. She thought that the students were being unkind to Abigail. In the recess that day, she smiled at Abigail. But Abigail didn't respond and left with her tray.

Katniss was a bit shocked. She was a good-natured girl who had many friends. Everyone loved to be her friend. But Abigail had just plainly ignored her. She didn't think much about that unusual incident. Next day Katniss went to the Cape Town Middle School in Australia. During the 15 days of her stay there, she made many new friends. Everyone was kind and gentle. She loved them. On her last day, her new friends promised to keep in touch via phone or Facebook.

When she returned to her class, she was shocked to see that Abigail was still sitting alone. No one seemed to acknowledge her presence. During the lunch, a girl dropped her tray. Spontaneously Abigail rushed forward to help her but the girl just glared at Abigail and went away. Katniss asked her best friend why no one was talking to Abigail. Her friend laughed and quipped, "Who would talk to such a person?"

Katniss was hurt. She had received such a warm treatment in another country and here her own friends were ignoring Abigail.

She picked up her books and went to Abigail's seat. She smiled and asked, "May I sit here with you?"

Abigail was shocked to hear such words from the most popular girl of the school. She smiled and said, "Yes, if you want to."

Katniss sat with Abigail the whole day and discovered that she was a very sweet girl. The two became friends right away.

That afternoon after school, Katniss's friends cornered her and asked her, "What has happened to you? Why are you talking to her? You don't care about your reputation. You are the most popular girl in the school. What would everyone say if they saw you talking to her?"

Katniss got angry and told them how she was treated at the other school. She retorted, "I care about my reputation that's why I am talking to her. I don't want to be called a racist and insensitive."

Her friends were speechless for a moment. She continued her passionate lecture, "Only illiterate people discriminate. Civilized people don't. You all call yourselves modern and cool. But do you realize how modern your actions are? You have such an outdated thinking. Just imagine if I were black, would you all stop talking to me? May be I don't know. Abigail is a very good girl. She is my friend and will remain so. And if you don't want to talk to her, you can stop talking to me as well."

Her angry outburst made everyone speechless. Her friends realized their mistake and were ashamed of their actions. The next day they all said sorry to Abigail, and asked her to become their friend. Abigail forgave them, and all of them became good friends.

Give-and-Take Session

Prejudice is an unfair and usually a negative attitude. Prejudice is contagious as it is passed from one person to another or from one group to another. In modern society, prejudice of any kind is rooted in ignorance.

Racism is a kind of prejudice where you think one race is superior and others are inferior. Racism is hatred against another based on their skin color, culture and religion. Racism often breeds fear and hatred. It is a destructive disease. The concept of race was born out of narrow-mindedness.

Today we all know that racial discrimination is bad. But that was not the case in the 18th and 19th century. Some ignorant people still justify their racial misconduct by pointing out that many American presidents owned slaves and believed in slavery. While it may be partly true, it has to be seen in a relational context of that age and generation.

In the 17th century, the term 'race' was originally used to categorize humans. In the 18th century, some people, who were interested in controlling others, began to attach color and cultural values to race. Later this approach was used to justify slavery and segregation in the United States, apartheid in the Republic of South Africa and colonialism and imperialism in Europe.

Many American presidents owned slaves. Some even while they were in office. But the last president to own slaves was the eighteenth president, Ulysses S. Grant (1869-1877). Historians justify it because it was required at that time for economic and other reasons. In today's context it is wrong. But when they did it, it was a common practice. It wasn't considered wrong as per the general trend of thought during that period of time. In 1858, even Lincoln said "I am in favor of having the superior position assigned to the white race." However, later Lincoln was clearly opposed to slavery. Here it is important to note that the American founders had opposed slavery on principle and tolerated it only from necessity.

Points to Ponder
(It is not necessary for students to answer the questions or participate in discussion. They are just required to ponder over them. So, after every question or statement, a brief pause is recommended so as to allow their subconscious mind to absorb the desired values.)

- Why Katie ignored Abigail?
- Was it Abigail's fault that she was born in Africa?

- When Katniss smiled at Abigail, why Abigail ignored her?
- Why Katniss wanted to sit with Abigail?
- To make people more caring to members of other groups, they should be subjected to similar harsh treatment. Do you agree?
- By imaging themselves in the same situation, people can gain a greater understanding of other people's humiliation. Do you agree?
- Why is it important to preserve, develop and appreciate different cultures?

Nelson Mandela is the most noteworthy leader who stood against racism and apartheid. His words, "the struggle is my life", give a glimpse of his fierce determination to fight against racism and discrimination. Mandela was awarded the Nobel Peace Prize in 1993 for his struggle. These words from his statement to the court, sum up his guiding principles: "During my lifetime I have dedicated myself to this struggle of the African people. I have fought against white domination, and I have fought against black domination. I have cherished the ideal of a democratic and free society in which all persons live together in harmony and with equal opportunities. It is an ideal which I hope to live for and to achieve. But if needs be, it is an ideal for which I am prepared to die."

As human beings, we are all more alike than we are different, regardless of the color of our skin. And the genetic analysis of humans has proved this. Research shows that there is so much genetic overlap between groups formerly designated as races that the term 'race' is meaningless and biologically unwarranted. Remember, racism is an outdated concept that is still embraced by the ignorant, the intolerant and those who can't accept change.

Finally, remember the words of Hellen Keller: "The highest result of education is tolerance."

26. The Secret of Happiness

Purpose of the module: It is intended to make the students aware that helping others lead to happiness and contentment. At the same time, the students should also realize the importance of time and manage it wisely to succeed in this ever competitive world. While excessive screen time may help children pass time, but it can be a potential source of depression, stress and boredom afterwards because time spent on TV, mobile, computer, etc. leads to little or no gratification.

Key Values: Helpfulness, Friendship.
Supplementary Values: Gratitude, Caring.
Life Skills: Time Management, Good Habits.
Estimated Storytelling Time: 5 to 7 Minutes
Give-and-Take Session: 6 to 10 Minutes

Cody was in the 6th grade. He got bored easily. He was always unhappy no matter what he did. Happiness always seemed to elude him, no matter how much he tried to be happy. He had lovely parents, nice teachers and great friends, and he also had all the latest gadgets, still he was unhappy. His performance in the school was reasonably good. Yet, he never felt satisfied with life. When he watched TV, he got bored within half an hour. Then he used to surf the internet, there also he would get bored very soon. Even playing with his friends didn't give him much happiness. He was very confused. He tried hard to search the secret of happiness, but this secret seemed to be too secretive.

He noticed that his friend Cage was always happy. Cage got same grades and had same friends but he always seemed to be happy. He never got bored easily. He would find interesting pastimes easily.

Cody decided to talk to Cage and ask him about the secret of happiness. He went to Cage and asked, "How is that you are always happy. Please tell me the secret of happiness. I am tired of searching it. I am starting to believe that I am a born pessimist. Perhaps because of my blood group that is B negative."

Cage was surprised to hear such an unusual request. He thought for a while. He carefully analyzed the question and finally admitted, "I don't know the secret of happiness. You are right. I am always happy but I can't tell you why. I have always been this way. I have always done the same things. You are my good friend, and I want to help you. Why don't you come and stay with me for a day? I don't know the secret, but maybe you can observe me and discover it on your own."

Cody replied, "Thanks a lot for your offer Cage. I will ask mom and let you know whenever I can come over."

Next weekend, Cody's parents had to visit a distant relative. Cody asked them if he could stay with Cage on the weekend. They agreed.

Cody went to Cage's home and started observing his every movement. As they were walking back from the market, an old lady was crossing the road. Cody got irritated by waiting for her and lightly pushed her aside to cross the road. He turned back as Cage was not beside him. He was astonished to see that Cage was helping that lady cross the road as the traffic was heavy. He remembered Cage's action. Then after lunch, as Cage's mother was taking dishes to the kitchen sink, Cage got up and offered, "May I do the dishes mom?"

His mother kissed his forehead and said, "You are such a good boy Cage. You clean the dishes while I'll get the groceries."

As Cage was cleaning, Cody also went to help him. Together they completed the work in 10 minutes and Cody felt happy to help Cage.

At night as he was getting ready to sleep, he noticed that Cage was sitting on his porch and gazing at the stars. Cody went and asked him, "What are you doing here?"

Cage replied, "I am thinking about my day and my today's schedule. And I am counting all those people that I made smile today. Remembering their smiles makes me happy. I feel gratified, as I have done a good deed."

Whole night Cody thought over on the wise words of his sage friend. He coined a phrase for his wise friend and planned to tell all his friends that 'Cage is a Sage at this Age' and laughed heartily. Cody realized that his life lacked gratification. Gratification leads to happiness so in order to be truly happy he needs to find gratification first. He must make others happy. Then only, he can be happy himself.

From then on, Cody started helping others whenever he could. His mother was happy to see him doing household chores. Seeing her happy, he felt a strange kind of happiness. He began to understand the true meaning of happiness. He also found a cure for his boredom. Whenever he was free, he helped others. Now his life was happy and hopeful, and he began enjoying every moment of it.

Give-and-Take Session

Happiness is something that everybody is searching for. When you are happy, life just feels great. Everything feels good. Everyone wants to find a shortcut to happiness. But very few realize that helping someone else is the shortcut to feeling good.

Ancient wisdom has always taught the importance of helping others. Now research has confirmed that this is indeed the way to feel good about yourself. Several studies show that helping others lowers stress levels, while increasing happiness. And helping others is good for your health too.

In a recent test aimed at measuring the happiness and spending habits, some people were monitored before and after they received a bonus of over $3,000. The results that emerged clearly showed that those who spend money on others are far happier than those who spend it on themselves.

And it is not about money only. If you have more time than money, you can still make a big difference in others lives by donating your time. This could be a great way for many people as it provides an outlet to meet and help others. The happiness of oneself, i.e., self-fulfillment and happiness of others, i.e., self-sacrifice are inseparable. Selfless giving to others is really rewarding, as it leads to the satisfaction of making a difference. The renowned Harvard psychologist David McClelland found that just thinking about helping others seems to have a positive physiological impact.

But then, it is important to know that, just as excessive focus on self (i.e., self-fulfillment) may be unhealthy, an excessive focus on others (i.e., self-sacrifice) may be unhealthy as well. Like all things, you have to keep it in balance. Balance is obviously a very important part of our lives and needs to be maintained in all aspects.

Points to Ponder

- Why Cody used to feel sad and depressed after watching TV or surfing internet for some time?
- What was the secret of Cage's happiness?
- Why Cody was laughing after coining the phrase 'Cage is a Sage at this Age'? Do you think he was planning to write a poem on Cage?
- Some studies confirm that people who spend their money on others were happier than people who spend their money on themselves. Why?
- Do you think people aspire to become politicians so as to get a chance to help others? Why?
- Helping others leads to positive thoughts which in turn leads to positive energy and happiness. Do you agree?
- Can spending more than your spare time in helping others leads to unhappiness? Why?
- How thinking about helping others can have a positive impact on our mood?

- How can I help others, particularly when I myself need help?
- Why time management and balance are important in our life?

Many studies confirm that volunteering or helping others is a great antidote to the boredom. It is not that the studies confirming the benefits of volunteering relate only to older adults. The studies of younger people show that they also get the similar benefits. It has been documented that volunteering in adolescence enhances social competence and self-esteem, protects against anti-social behaviors and academic failure. What's more, the benefits of starting young appear to bring lifelong benefits.

In your pursuit of happiness, learn by heart the words of Nobel Peace Prize winner Dr. Albert Schweitzer, "The only ones among you who will be really happy are those who have sought and found how to serve."

27. The Las Vegas Trip

Purpose of the Module: The objective is to remind children about selfless, unconditional love of parents for their children who often take them for granted and show no appreciation for their efforts. Children should realize that while good friends are important, their family members also need love and respect. And it ought to be a two-way traffic. They should appreciate that while a bit of naughtiness may be acceptable, but risky behaviors like substance abuse and violence are to be avoided at all costs.

Key Values: Respect for Parents, Avoiding Drugs.
Supplementary Values: Obedience, Managing Peer pressure, Appreciating the Family Love.
Life Skills: Good Habits, Flexibility, Self-control, Discipline.
Estimated Storytelling Time: 5 to 7 Minutes
Give-and-Take Session: 5 to 10 Minutes

David was a good boy at school, but very naughty at home. He was very intelligent for his age. His father was a software engineer. And his stepmother was a doctor. While he was friendly with everyone, sometimes he behaved stubbornly and insisted on doing things his way. He would become angry when any of his demands were not met immediately. And then he would not listen to anyone; he would do his own thing.

Once, some boys of his street planned a trip to Las Vegas during the summer break. Everyone was very excited. They would talk about this trip all the time. They asked David to join them. David was also tempted to join them on this fun trip.

David asked his mother but she didn't give him permission. He tried to argue but she was relentless. He was very annoyed. Finally, he lost his temper and said, "I know you are my step mom. That's why you can't see me happy."

His father was shocked to hear this. He scolded David for his behavior. But David was behaving as if he was not listening. He was unapologetic and acted like there was nothing wrong.

David went to his room and slammed the door shut. He was cursing his luck when suddenly he got a Facebook alert on his phone. His friend Justin had sent him a message. Justin also lived in the same street. But he was not going on the trip, as his grandfather was ill. David was not in a mood for any conversation. Yet, he messaged Justin that he hated his mother and he too was not going to Las Vegas.

David was stunned to read Justin's reply. Justin conveyed him that his grandfather's health was an excuse because he didn't want to go. He knew some of those boys used drugs and that's why he was not going. David was shocked. He didn't know those boys were into drugs. He felt disgusted and horrified at the thought of going on a trip with such boys.

In a flash, David realized his mistake. He was deeply regretting his behavior, but he was confused as to what to do about it. He felt his head spinning when he recalled his harsh words. He was at a complete loss as to what to do next.

When he couldn't bear it anymore, he dashed to the kitchen where his mother was preparing the dinner. He told her everything about Justin's message. Then he hugged her and whispered, "I am sorry mom. Please forgive me."

His mother hugged him back and said, "David I knew that. And because of this reason, I am not sending you with them. I love you, and as a mother, I always have to keep your best interests in my mind."

His father also embraced him tightly and remarked, "Other parents don't spend enough time with their kids. That's why the kids get spoilt. Instead of time, they spend money on their children. Such parents equate success with money. But we have a different definition of success. We want you to be happy in life. That is why we will always do what's best for you in the long run. And as far as Vegas trip is concerned, your mother has already asked me to plan a trip there in summer holidays."

David was very happy to hear this. He thanked God for giving him such a caring mother.

Give-and-Take Session

We often hear comments, complaints or compliments from parents that their child is well-behaved at school but naughty at home. Some parents may not be happy about it, but we, the teachers are usually happy about it. Not because it makes our work a bit easier. But for the fact that children, who are well-behaved at school but naughty at home, are typically strongly bonded to their family and know they can afford to be carefree and relaxed at home.

In school, the average student is glued to his or her desk for almost seven hours a day. Children need to unwind after seven hours of school. In fact, they deserve a carefree and informal environment at home. And parents should be happy that they are providing a safe, secure and relaxed environment to their children where they can freely express themselves or even take a bit of liberty. A home where children feel loved and comfortable enough to express what they are feeling is good for children's growth and development. They feel important as they know their opinions and ideas are more valued at home where it is not a 1 in 20 situation as in the school.

And if children behave badly or act up occasionally and realize it in time, it is good for the children also. Perhaps, it is good to be a bit bad sometimes. They learn the ways of the world. But then, balance is the key, especially for morally weak children. We have to keep in mind that children have to go through growing up phases. And in this touch-screen world, growing up is tough enough. Then again, we should keep in mind that every family and every child is completely different so there is really no standard way to perfectly deal with behavior issues.

Points to Ponder

- Why David was naughty at home but well-behaved at school?
- Why David's mother didn't give him the permission for the Las Vegas trip?
- David said to her mother, "I know you are my step mom. That's why you can't see me happy." Was he venting his anger or just emotionally blackmailing his mother?
- How David realized his mistake?
- Why David was in a hurry to say sorry to his mom? Do you think he should have waited to see whether his mom gives permission as a result of his rash comments?
- Have you ever hurt your father or mother? When you realize your folly, do you try to make them happy? If no, why? If yes, how?
- Being a mother is a state of mind, an attitude of caring and loving unconditionally. Do you agree?
- Children should understand the value and importance of relationships as early as possible. What do you think?
- We all know the fact that one should hate the sin and not the sinner. Then why David's mother and Justin's parents were reluctant to send their children with those boys who take drugs?
- Maintaining school discipline is important. Punishments are often necessary to teach the value of disciplined behavior to transform carefree children into productive adults. What are your views about discipline?

President Abraham Lincoln once wrote a letter as a parent, to his son's teacher requesting him what to teach to his son. Here is a relevant excerpt from that letter.

Respected Teacher

My son will have to learn, I know, that all men are not just, all men are not true. But teach him also that for every scoundrel there is a hero; that for every selfish politician, there is a dedicated leader. Teach him that for every enemy there is a friend...

Try to give my son the strength not to follow the crowd when everyone is getting on the bandwagon.

Teach him to listen to all men but teach him also to filter all he hears on a screen of truth and take only the good that comes through...

Treat him gently; but do not cuddle him because only the test of fire makes fine steel.

I repeat.

Treat him gently; but do not cuddle him because only the test of fire makes fine steel.

28. A Story of Story Books

Purpose of the Module: This section is designed to encourage reading habits among students. They should realize that books have a long track record of success in imparting knowledge and wisdom. But we cannot say that for newer channels. While the e-media have many pros and cons, they are yet to prove their worth. So, a balanced approach is the right way to go.

Key Values: Quest for Knowledge, Democratic Decision Making.
Supplementary Values: Perseverance, Balance, Team Spirit, Imagination.
Life Skills: Problem Solving, Initiative, Creative Thinking.
Estimated Storytelling Time: 6 to 8 Minutes
Give-and-Take Session: 6 to 11 Minutes

The science teacher, Mr. Harrison, met with a nasty accident, which left his right leg permanently damaged. So the school authorities made him the librarian.

Mr. Harrison was a big fan of electronic books and video games. He was a tech freak. His Facebook and Twitter profiles were a proof of this fact. Now he was not teaching science, but he still wanted to propagate science among students. So he stopped issuing fiction books to students. When the students asked for fairy tales or magic books, he told them that these books were against science, and they should not read such filth. He gave various reasons, such as in the 21st century students should learn to be realistic. They should not be fascinated by dark fantasies like the Harry Potter series and the Twilight series. If they like fiction, they could read science fiction in the digital format. It would help them to imagine futuristic things.

Moreover, Mr. Harrison introduced e-books and video games in the library. He informed everyone, "Digital books and video games are environment friendly. I recommend e-books of science fiction and real life stories for inspiration. And I strongly recommend video games to develop mental skills such as attention, memory, visual and auditory processing and thinking. Computer games enhance reflexes and other reactions of the brain... Video games also improve skills such as high-level thinking, reflexes and concentration. They also help to promote animation, programming and other computer skills among youngsters. And computer skills are important to succeed in life." He finished his passionate preaching after half an hour.

Most girls of the school were very upset with the new changes. The girls of sixth grade sent an email to J. K. Rowling but they didn't get any reply as she was too busy writing her new novel of Barry after her blockbuster novels of Harry. Then they decided to contact professor Dumbledore but it was impossible to trace him, not to talk of writing a letter to him. Then they realized that wishful thinking won't help. So, they decided to take the matter in their own hands.

Fortunately for them, there was an open competition in which students had to make a PowerPoint presentation regarding their hobbies. They also had to explain the role of their chosen hobby on the holistic development of children. All the girls of the sixth grade formed a group, and decided to make a presentation titled 'A Story of Story Books.' They divided the topic into eight parts namely: positive entertainment, getting smarter, improving concentration, developing creativity & thinking skills, improving writing skills, appreciating emotions, improving attitudes & character, and disadvantages of books. Each girl got one part.

The girls referred many studies to prove their points. They established that story books have many emotional and psychological benefits. They used many scientific studies and research to prove their claims. They worked hard for two weeks and did lots of research and analysis to complete their presentation.

The panel of judges included Mr. Harrison. Some girls got worried as their presentation was against Mr. Harrison's views. They were sure to lose. But they had faith in each other and their cause. They had worked hard for it, and they were confident of their ideas. With confidence, they delivered an effective presentation.

The whole school applauded them for such a great presentation. But the big surprise came in the form of Mr. Harrison's speech. He got up and called them on the stage. Then he said, "I have a confession to make. I was against fiction. Now I am not. My thinking was wrong. I was biased. Now I am not. In fact, now you all will see me propagating books, particularly story books. Because of these little girls, now I can see things in the right perspective. They had faith in their cause, and the courage to prove it. Surely, this is something they learnt from reading fiction. Ok now enough of my blabbering. Now I request Principal Sir to announce the names of the winners."

The Principal announced, "The results are no surprise. 'A Story of Story Books' has been adjudged the best presentation on hobbies. I congratulate the girls from the sixth grade. These little fairies have won the competition. As for their prize, earlier it was a set of latest videogames but now they will also get a set of latest books on fairytales, magic, etc."

Give-and-Take Session

In this day and age of digital world, books are losing their fun factor. And the worrying point is that children are not reading as much as they should. They are spending most of their time viewing television shows, surfing web, playing video games and all that.

Nowadays many children do not appreciate that reading is an important part of our life. They do not have time for books; they are too busy in their digital world. They do not realize, or do not want to realize that if they do not read enough, they will not reach their full potential. Books are losing their appeal, but not the importance.

Remember, almost all successful people have one thing in common. They enjoyed a good dose of good books in their childhood. Be it Benjamin Franklin, Aristotle, Shakespeare, Thomas Jefferson, Mark Twain, Leonardo Da Vinci, Thomas Edison, Theodore Roosevelt, Albert Einstein, Andrew Carnegie, and the rest, they all had personal libraries. They loved books. They were avid readers.

Even today's political and business leaders read many books every month. While they are the busiest people managing nations or mega businesses, still they read much more than an average person. No wonder they earn at least 100 times more than an average person.

Points to Ponder

- Why Mr. Harrison was promoting video games. Do you agree with him?
- How did the girls prove that fiction is good for kids?
- Recall three reasons why you love fiction.
- What do you think are the benefits of fiction? Do e-books offer all these benefits?
- Can you imagine a life without fiction?
- Printed books are not environment friendly. Do you agree?
- People have been using paper books for centuries. But environmental issues have assumed alarming proportions in the last few decades. Incidentally, the e-media have become popular in the last few decades. Do you find any connection?
- How do you maintain balance between reading and other pastime activities?
- We often hear the words like tech addict, TV addict and net addict, but rarely hear the word book addict. Why book addiction is not usually considered a disease?

Many studies show that children are spending more and more time on digital media. But they are not keeping up their share of reading time. It is gradually coming down even if we include digital books. The governments and educators all over the world are doing their best to encourage reading among children. But more and more children are finding digital media more interesting than books. It seems many of them are trapped in the World Wide Web.

Still a day has 24 hours. And children, perhaps emulating adults, consider it cool to engage with the new digital media. They find it more tempting than books. Since ages, books have been a proven way to succeed in life. But the impact of these new channels on the growth of children is still not clear. On the other hand, the power of books is time tested.

Books have many psychological benefits. They give wings to thoughts. They give solace and solutions to kids with problems. Healthy fiction inspires everyone. Most stories end on a positive note and as such encourage people to be optimistic in life. Good books encourage readers to face the difficulties of life head on. And the best advantage that fiction has over science is that it allows exploration of ideas without negative consequences. What's more, many studies confirm that fiction has a good effect on one's soul. So, cultivate a habit for reading; it will make you more valuable.

In today's world, both books and e-media are indispensable to succeed in life. Like in all walks of life, here also maintaining balance is the key to success.

29. What's the Matter?

Purpose of the Module: This section is planned to make children realize that good habits are very important to their happiness, well-being and success. They should also realize that responsibility includes taking care of others, not just taking care of their own needs. Children should know that all members of a family have their roles and responsibilities to perform. And they can strengthen their family by making sure that all family members have a clear idea about their day-to-day responsibilities in and to the family.

Key Values: Responsibility to Family and Self, Discipline.
Supplementary Values: Self-reliance, Helpfulness, Unconditional Love.
Life Skills: Self-help, Time Management, Organizing.
Estimated Storytelling Time: 6 to 8 Minutes
Give-and-Take Session: 6 to 10 Minutes

"Sorry Ma'am, I am late," Fred said while entering the class with a sleepy face. Everyone stared at Fred. He was in a complete mess. His hair was not properly combed, his tie was missing and the back of his shirt had become partially untucked. Fred was carrying his notebooks in his hand while his bag was open, with some of the books hanging out of the bag. The teacher stared at Fred in disbelief. Her expression indicated as if she was wondering what happened, but she just nodded and signaled him to take his seat.

Fred asked Jordan for a pencil as he forgot his pencil box at home. Jordan was surprised because normally Fred was always on time and never forgot his things. Jordan asked Fred, "What's the matter. You are always well organized. What happened today?"

Fred told him that his mother was not well. He had to take care of her and his baby sister, Ginny. Doctor had told mother not to go near Ginny because she was suffering from the infectious flu. So it was his responsibility to take care of Ginny. He was finding it difficult to manage on his own. His mother used to run after them day and night taking care of him and Ginny. Now without her, he was in a mess. He didn't study a bit yesterday as he had gone out to play, and no one called him back.

Fred narrated everything in detail to Jordan. He said, "You know what happened yesterday. I went out to play. I lost the track of time and returned late. Ginny was crying at that time. I forgot to feed her before I went out. When I came back, mother was preparing milk for Ginny. She was worried that Ginny could catch flu. You know it's not easy being a single parent. She worries about us all the time. Now she is suffering because of my neglect and irresponsibility as if she doesn't have enough to worry about at the moment."

Jordan sympathized, "So how is she doing now?"

Fred replied, "I don't know. Yesterday night my aunt came and she took mother and Ginny to her place. She asked me to come along, but I had to refuse. I was very embarrassed because of my carelessness. And then and there I decided to change my habits. Now I would do all my chores myself and learn how to take some responsibility for my family. So today morning, I tried to do everything but it was the first time in my life that I had to do so many things on my own at one time. I forgot to iron my dress and pack my bag yesterday night. So I had to hurry throughout the morning. Even then, I got late. I wonder how mother could do all the things at the same time."

Jordan cleared his throat a bit self-importantly and said, "How you take responsibility in life is more important than anything else. What sets you apart as a responsible person is how you plan your things and how you care for your family. So, why don't you plan your things and do them accordingly. You can arrange all your school things on the previous night itself. That way you can attend to other things in the morning. And why don't you get up half an hour early to help your mother when she comes back? It will help her recover quickly. Remember, you have to prove that you're responsible! After all how we take responsibility for family members makes life fulfilling."

After a week when Fred's mother came back, she was surprised to see that Fred was taking good care of himself and everything was spic-and-span in the house. She smiled through her tears and said, "I always treated you as a little kid and didn't let you do chores. But I didn't know that you have become a big boy, a responsible boy. Now I am finding it difficult to believe that you are the same boy who used to take credit for all things and blame my upbringing for all your faults."

Fred was very happy to see the tears rolling down from his mother's eyes. He knew that those were tears of joy.

Give-and-Take Session

We know that every child is full of promise and potential. What is not always clear is how to help each child reach that potential. What makes one child a 'smarty' and another a permanent 'struggler'? What makes one child develop into a leader and another not? What makes one child healthier than another child?

Childhood years are the most formative and impressionable years in one's life. We all know that early influences greatly affect a child's ability to learn and succeed in life. It is very true that the habits we acquire in our childhood remain with us throughout our lives. And it is important to understand the role of habits acquired during the impressionable age on lifelong results. In a time of accelerating change, it is more important than ever before. Otherwise, it could prove quite damaging in these rapidly changing environments where newer technologies are penetrating the protective walls of homes and schools.

Good habits develop our personality and make us a lovable person. Our habits greatly affect our lives, but we often take them for granted. Sometimes we don't even realize we have developed a habit, good or bad. They are formed through our thoughts, attitudes, and ultimately, our actions.

It has justly been said that 'man is a bundle of habits'. Our habits make us who we are. The key is to control habits. If we know how to change our habits, then even a minor effort can create major results.

Good habits are also called the right way to live. Right from the way of living to the choices one person makes, it reflects a personality. And the good thing about developing positive habits is that they can become a natural part of our personality. We begin to do them without thinking about them. They become a second nature. But this is also true of bad habits. It's important that we should learn how to shed the bad habits and replace them with good ones that will serve us forever.

Points to Ponder

- Fred used to take credit for any good thing. Was it fair on his part to blame his mother's role in raising him for his mistakes?
- Success is not an accident; success is a good habit. How are good habits and success connected?
- How can you become more responsible for your own learning and future?
- How do you become a smart family? How do you show responsibility at home?
- What place does your family hold in your life? What place do you hold in your family?
- What responsibilities do you now have for your family members?
- How does a person learn to be responsible?
- What happens in relationships when a person is not responsible?
- Are you letting bad habits rule your life? Why?
- Responsibility to yourself means that you don't fall for shallow and easy solutions. Do you agree?
- What are the outcomes of being irresponsible? How can you assume more responsibility for yourself and your family?

Remember, responsibility means doing what needs to be done to take care of yourself, your family and your friends. And it's simply a choice that you have to make.

Life consists of each day. Every day is important in your life. Make it a point to learn at least one new thing each day. And don't forget to take responsibility for the little things today too. Don't delay it. Developing good habits that will help you succeed can never start too early.

Good habits will help you create success for the rest of your life. In the beginning, you may find it a bit difficult. Remember, taking responsibility is not something you master over the weekend. So you might as well get started with it right now.

Aristotle beautifully described the importance of good habits for children by saying: "Good habits formed at youth make all the difference."

30. A Twitter Conversation with God

Purpose of the Module: The objective is to acquaint the students about the pros and cons of e-media and constant multitasking. They should be encouraged to appreciate the importance of time and know how to use it wisely. They should identify their major time-wasters (TV, internet, music, phone, games, etc.) and make a plan to control them intelligently.

Key Values: Proper Utilization of Time, Self-discipline.
Supplementary Values: Balance, Regularity.
Life Skills: Self-help, Time Management, Organizing.
Estimated Storytelling Time: 6 to 8 Minutes
Give-and-Take Session: 6 to 8 Minutes

Tom Dreat is scared. His exams start next week, and he has not started studying yet. His dad has promised him a PlayStation if he gets an 'A' grade. But what if he gets his usual 'C' grade? He is really worried and unable to focus on studies. He wishes someone could pull him out of this mess. He needs help more than ever now, and he feels that only God can help him now. So he decides to contact God on his favorite Twitter channel to seek divine help.

Tom tweeted: God, please help me. My exams are coming and I have not studied. Kindly help me.

God retweeted: Do you want me to study and write your papers?

Tom: Is that possible?

God: Yes, I am a good learner. I can help you only if you can send your printed study material to the heaven. You see, I am not comfortable with these e-readers and iPads. Besides, I find them distracting.

Tom: Sorry God, our courier companies do not cover heaven. Is there any other way? Why don't you come here and appear on my behalf?

God: Yes, I can come if you can ensure that no honest person sees me there. You know, I am a shy person. Besides, I'm afraid what will happen to my reputation if any honest person sees me in the act?

Tom: How can I do that? That's impossible.

God: Then how can I help you?

Tom: I don't know. You are God, and you are supposed to help people in trouble. Just a minute! Let me change my song list on the iPod.

God: Are you listening music right now?

Tom: Yeah. I have to do two or more things at the same time because you have given us only 24 hours in a day.

God: Yeah, everyone has 24 hours. I am an equal opportunity provider. You are a student, and a student is supposed to study regularly.

Tom: God, here again you are at fault. Why have you given me the dumb genes? I have to study hours and hours to complete the course.

God: Yeah, I know. My job is to make a distinction between good and bad, deserving and non-deserving, hard working and hardly working people. To err is human and sometimes, I behave like a human.

Tom: Are you saying I am not a hard working person? I am a very hard working boy. You see, I just sleep for five hours, sometimes even less.

God: I know you sleep for five hours. Your account also shows that you usually spend 5 hours on the internet, 2 hours on the mobile, 5 hours on TV and some time on video games.

Tom: ...
Message from Twitter "Requests exceeded but may continue as a special case"

Tom: Dear God, why don't you ask Zuck to make Facebook like Twitter, but with no restrictions? Don't you feel that Twitter is very 'limiting' because of the hourly limit and characters limit?

God: In heaven, Twitter offers a flexible limit as we don't squeeze the words. By the way, who is this Zuck?

Tom: Mark Zuckerberg, the creator of Facebook.

God: Oh, Mark. But he is roaming in China with Chan, and Facebook is banned there.

Tom: But, why China of all the places.

God: Perhaps, he is running away from the Facebook since he knows the secret of success. It just reminds me that you always remember me just before the exams. I can show you the way to succeed if you call me after the exams.

Tom: In future, I will call you after exams if you help me this time.

God: You are not supposed to put conditions on God. It's not the first exam you're taking. And this one won't be the last. Study, prepare and then relax. And confidently take the test. I repeat, I will tell you the success secret if you call me after the exams. Good luck for now!

After a week, Tom tweeted again: God, you promised that next time I would get a PlayStation.

God retweeted: A PlayStation. What's that?

God: Oh, no you just promised to tell me Zuck's secrets.

God: Yeah, it just occurred to me that Tom Dreat is just two steps away from becoming Great.

Tom: And what are these two steps?

God: First, I daily credit 1440 minutes to your account. Make good use of your daily balance. Remember, it cannot be carried over. The clock is running. Make the most of your 1440 minutes. Invest your time well so that you get from it what really matters to you.

Tom: So, proper utilization of time is the first point. And the second point?

God: Understand your priorities, and then concentrate on what really matters to you. That means focus on 'what you need to do' and not on 'what you want to do'. Tom *Dreat*, you can become *Great* just by limiting your unproductive time on TV, internet, mobile, etc. Now your Twitter time is over. Bless you.

Give-and-Take Session

Nowadays children spend more time with e-media than in any other activity. And the media have a big influence on children through the Internet, television, ads, games, music, movies, and many other ways. What's more, just to squeeze all this in their schedule, they become multitaskers. They study with music playing and the television on. They have conversations through text with a friend while simultaneously having dinner with family.

While this might sound like a good thing, it also means that children's attention spans are getting shorter and shorter. And children feel they are making the most of their time while juggling several activities at the same time. They enjoy multitasking; they feel good when their mind craves the 'high' of continuous, excessive excitement. But unfortunately, the research suggests that multitaskers are typically less efficient, less accurate, less competent, and less able to recall the content of what they have been doing compared to singletaskers.

There are some activities we can do two or more at a time. But when it comes to mental activities that require focus or thought, we are actually not multitaskers. Dividing the brain's attention between two or more mental tasks negatively affects both quality and quantity.

In a study titled 'Generation M: Media in the Lives of 8-18 Year Olds,' the Henry J. Kaiser Foundation has pointed out that over the past five years, there has been a huge increase in media use as well as multitasking among children. (They're calling this generation, Generation M for all the time they spend with e-media.) The study also observed that media use begets media use, that is, those young people who spend the most time using computers or playing video games also spend more time watching TV and listening to music. And multitasking certainly accounts for some of this.

Points to Ponder
(It is not necessary for students to answer the questions or participate in discussion. They are just required to ponder over them. So, after every question or statement, a brief pause is recommended so as to allow their subconscious mind to absorb the desired values.)

- Why Tom contacted God?
- Was Tom more interested in getting a PlayStation5 or good grades?
- Tom thought he had dumb genes. Was he right in thinking so?
- Why Tom blamed God for his dumb genes?
- Tom used to sleep for five hours, and he always try to do two things simultaneously like he was listening to music while conversing with God. Do you think he was a hard working boy?
- God gave 1440 minutes per day to everyone. Don't you think God should give more time to dumb people and less time to intelligent people?

- Tom used to watch TV or listen to music even while studying. Do you think this could be the reason for his poor grades?
- Do you multi-task when you study?
- Why God wanted Tom to focus on 'what he needs to do' and not on 'what he wants to do'?
- Do your habits help you achieve good results, or do they hinder your progress?
- Positive habits help you get what you want while negative habits hold you back. Do you agree?

It is no surprise that we do better work when we focus on one thing at a time without distractions. But, a new research by Stanford University points to something more serious. It confirms that people who spend long periods of time multi-tasking might lose their ability to pay attention, control their memory, or switch from one task to another. What's more, they can even lose the ability to multi-task as well. And these experiments were conducted on people who are used to multitasking and regularly deal with several streams of e-media at the same time.

It is very easy to get what you want when your habits work with you rather than against you. Remember that time waits for no one. Yesterday is history. Tomorrow is mystery. Today is a gift. That's why it's called the present!

Appendix A: Module wise Value Links

Module	Key Values	Supplementary Values
1. The Crying Girl	Compassion, Sense of Social Responsibility	Empathy, Presence of Mind, Courtesy
2. Brain Is King, Heart Is Queen	Sense of Good and Bad, Family Love	Empathy, Compassion, Peace
3. The Career Dilemma	Forward Looking, Humility	Responsibility to Self, Integrity, Sense of Right and Wrong
4. The Story of Sir Tory	Caring For Elders, Gratitude	Reverence for Old Age, Duty
5. An Echo from the Past	Responsibility to Parents, Unconditional Love	Gratitude, Tolerance, Humanism
6. The Perils of Plagiarism	Integrity, Quest for knowledge	Avoiding Plagiarism, Truthfulness, Kindness to Animals
7. A Trip to the Zoo	Healthy Eating, Positive Thinking	Healthy Living, Willpower, Kindness to Animals
8. The Winner's Way	Quest for Knowledge, Perseverance, Abstinence	Forward Looking, Duty, Self-discipline, Willpower
9. The Cause of the Pause	Friendship, Responsibility to Friends	Respect for the Environment, Self-discipline, Team Spirit
10. The Bully and the Beast	Knowing Oneself, Humility	Friendship, Modesty, Wisdom
11. Beautiful Betty	Healthy Living, Balance	Healthy Eating, Simple Living, Self-esteem
12. To Wear or Not To Wear	Responsibility to Self, Healthy Living	Managing Peer Pressure, Sense of Right and Wrong

Module	Key Values	Supplementary Values
13. Future We Don't Want	Respect for the Environment, Social Responsibility	Forward Looking, Common Cause, Simple Living
14. Runaways Never Win, Winners Never Run Away	Abstinence, Perseverance	Self-reliance, Faithfulness, Forgiveness
15. The Wrong Turn	Managing Peer Pressure Responsibility to Self, Sense of Right & Wrong	Self-reliance, Initiative
16. Every Day is Mother's Day	Responsibility to Family, Self-reliance, Caring	Cooperation, Initiative, Balance, Responsibility to Self
17. Was iPhone Worth It?	Sense of Right and Wrong, Managing Peer Pressure	Self-restraint, Simple Living
18. When Your Wish Comes True	Appreciating Fantasy vs. Reality, Sense of Right and Wrong	Obedience, Reasonableness, Self-restraint
19. What If I Crawl	Appreciating the Family Love, Managing Peer Pressure, Self-esteem	Sense of Right and Wrong, Self-motivation
20. The No-Gadget Trip	Appreciating the Family Love, Compassion	Sharing, Caring, Giving
21. The Art of Giving	Sense of Social Responsibility, Integrity	Honesty, Humanism, Kindness, Concern for others, Equality
22. Every Dog Has Its Way	Honesty, Avoiding Drugs	Kindness to Animals, Abstinence
23. Friend or Frenemy	Friendship, Integrity	Justice, Cooperation, Respect for the Environment, Sharing
24. Frog In A Well	Humility, Simple Living	Good Manners, Self-restraint, Friendship, Managing Peer Pressure
25. The True Friend	Tolerance, Equality	Humanism, Respect for Others, Cooperation, Dignity of Individual
26. The Secret of Happiness	Helpfulness, Friendship	Gratitude, Caring

Module	Key Values	Supplementary Values
27. The Las Vegas Trip	Respect for Parents, Avoiding Drugs	Appreciating the Family Love, Obedience, Managing Peer Pressure
28. A Story of Story Books	Quest for Knowledge, Democratic Decision Making	Perseverance, Balance, Imagination, Team Spirit
29. What's the Matter?	Responsibility to Family and Self, Discipline	Self-reliance, Helpfulness, Unconditional Love
30. A Twitter Conversation with God	Proper Utilization of Time, Self-discipline	Balance, Regularity

Appendix B: Module wise Life Skills & Estimated Session Times

Module	Life Skills	Est. Session Time for	
		Storytelling	Give-&-take
1. The Crying Girl	Courage, Initiative	6-8	5-9
2. Brain Is King, Heart Is Queen	Helpfulness, Initiative	6-8	5-10
3. The Career Dilemma	Self-awareness, Planning for the Future, Decision Making	7-9	5-10
4. The Story of Sir Tory	Tolerance, Respect for Elders, Flexibility	5-7	5-9
5. An Echo from the Past	Good Habits, Flexibility, Balance	5-8	6-11
6. The Perils of Plagiarism	Writing Skills, Hard Work, Self-help	5-8	6-9
7. A Trip to the Zoo	Thinking Skills, Good Habits, Self-control	5-8	6-10
8. The Winner's Way	Hard Work, Creative Thinking, Initiative, Devotion	5-8	5-9
9. The Cause of the Pause	Good Manners, Team Work, Self-control	5-7	6-8
10. The Bully and the Beast	Common Sense, Quest for Knowledge	6-8	6-8
11. Beautiful Betty	Healthy Body Image, Forward Looking, Good Manners	6-8	6-10
12. To Wear or Not To Wear	Self-awareness, Good Manners, Friendship	5-7	6-10

Module	Life Skills	Est. Session Time for	
		Storytelling	Give-&-take
13. Future We Don't Want	Cooperation, General Knowledge, Planning for the Future, Sharing	6-8	7-11
14. Runaways Never Win, Winners Never Run Away	Courage, Devotion, Forward Looking	6-8	7-12
15. The Wrong Turn	Decision Making, Career Planning	5-7	6-12
16. Every Day is Mother's Day	Time Management, Planning & Organizing, Discipline	6-8	6-12
17. Was iPhone Worth It?	Common Sense, Discipline	5-7	5-8
18. When Your Wish Comes True	Self-discipline, Willpower	5-8	5-9
19. What If I Crawl	Self-discipline, Will-power, Independence	6-8	6-10
20. The No-Gadget Trip	Balance, Self-control, Organizing	6-8	6-10
21. The Art of Giving	Caring, Sharing, Giving	5-7	6-8
22. Every Dog Has Its Way	Self-awareness, Integrity	4-6	6-9
23. Friend or Frenemy	Perseverance, Integrity, Hard Work	6-8	5-10
24. Frog In A Well	Willpower, Self-control, General Knowledge, Thriftiness	5-7	5-8
25. The True Friend	Fairness, Friendship, Good Manners	6-8	7-12
26. The Secret of Happiness	Time Management, Good Habits	5-7	6-10
27. The Las Vegas Trip	Good Habits, Flexibility, Self-control, Discipline	5-7	5-10

Module	Life Skills	Est. Session Time for	
		Storytelling	Give-&-take
28. A Story of Story Books	Problem Solving, Initiative, Creativity	6-8	6-11
29. What's the Matter?	Time Management, Organizing, Self-help	6-8	6-10
30. A Twitter Conversation with God	Time Management, Self-help, Organizing	6-8	6-8

NOTES

NOTES

NOTES

www.ingramcontent.com/pod-product-compliance
Lightning Source LLC
Chambersburg PA
CBHW070350090426
42733CB00009B/1363